Greenage. 81

FAITH

FAITH

Keith W. Clements

SCM PRESS LTD

334 00450 0

First published 1981
by SCM Press Ltd
58 Bloomsbury Street, London

Typeset by Gloucester Typesetting Co. Ltd
and printed in Great Britain by
Blackwell Press Ltd
Guildford and Worcester

Contents

Preface

The seed from which this book grew was a small weekend conference at a cottage in the Quantocks in November 1979, when I was invited by the Baptist and United Reformed Society of Bristol University to lead some study sessions on 'The Nature of Faith'. These students, who in their regular meetings had for some weeks been discussing the central items of Christian belief, evidently welcomed the opportunity to reflect upon faith itself, an issue which they felt they were in danger of taking for granted. For the initial stimulus which these future lawyers, doctors, teachers and scientists gave me in looking at the subject afresh, I am very grateful.

As for the soil in which the seed has grown, I hope I am not alone in feeling that in much recent theological discussion the basic issue of what it means to have faith has suffered some neglect. The debate about the incarnation, as a myth or otherwise, will doubtless continue for some time. On the other hand, voices are raised in protest at what is seen as a mere academic game, by those who stress Christianity as action, and theology as reflection upon action. Both understanding and action are integral to Christianity. But in the Christian context it is *faith* which seeks understanding, and which bears fruit in action. Without faith, there is nothing to understand, and nothing to act on. For these reasons, and for those outlined in the first chapter, no apology is offered for raising again a subject which may seem too obvious for serious discussion.

I have tried to present Christian faith in its wholeness, not simply as what the believer thinks, or feels, or does, but as nothing less than a personal relationship with God which involves the whole person. The thinking, the feeling, the doing, must not, as all too often happens, be divorced from this relationship. If the reader feels that what is said in the book has already been said one way or another, and much better, I am only too glad to be recognized as following in a well-worn track of Christian thought, both ancient and more recent, if it means that the importance of that route is being acknowledged anew. If he or she feels that the book raises as many questions as there are pages, that should not be surprising either, if we are dealing with what Kierkegaard called the supreme human passion.

Bristol Baptist College
June 1980

I

————— ✦ —————

Faith as a Question

'And you believe in God?'

By her tone of voice she clearly expected the answer 'Yes'. But
her look also conveyed a sense of wonderment, faced with a subject apparently quite outside the orbit of her usual concerns. Such
a simple question, yet it took me quite aback. Some few minutes
before, I had stopped the car to give this young woman and her
boyfriend a lift. It did not take long for them to reveal that they
were students returning to their polytechnic after a weekend in
London, and very little longer for them to elicit from me that I
was a minister on my way to a clergy retreat on the south Devon
coast. Neither had had any contact with any church that they
could remember, and as though suddenly presented with the
chance to talk with a living fossil, they began plying me with
questions about the job of a minister and the state of the churches
today. Soon, warming to their genuine interest I was into top
gear, holding forth on the fulfilments to be found through working with a Christian community, the role and relevance of the
ministry in modern society, and so on. Then, out of the blue, came
her question: 'And you believe in God?'

I caught my breath, because to her it obviously seemed that
'believing in God' was just another thing that went along with all
the other items of a minister's life, like taking services, visiting
the sick, chairing meetings and typing the church magazine. In
part, I was embarrassed on behalf of her naivety. How could she
possibly imagine that a minister, of all people, would do other
than 'believe in God' – and not as one among other activities, but
as the basis and motivation of them all?

But it was a healthy experience to face such an innocent question from someone who took nothing for granted, who saw faith as a rather odd business which not even a parson could be assumed to have. The background of her assumptions was rather like that of the girl Coral Musker in Graham Greene's *Stamboul Train*. The rationalistic atheist Dr Czinner, caught up with her in a desperate plight, notices her praying that her lover will come to her rescue.

> He spoke to her angrily: 'You are lucky to believe that that will do good,' but he found to his amazement that she could instinctively outbid his bitterness, which was founded on theories laboriously worked out by a fallible reason. 'I don't,' she said, 'but one must do something.'
>
> He was shocked by the ease of her disbelief, which did not come from the painful reading of rationalist writers and nineteenth century scientists, she had been born to disbelief as securely as he had been born to belief. He had sacrificed security in order to reach the same position, and for a moment he longed to sow in her some dry plant of doubt, a half-belief which would make her mistrust her judgement.[1]

My passenger did me a service in reminding me that faith *is* a peculiar affair, and the simple question was profoundly disturbing. I could be a busy minister in an active church, but I could still be asked: 'Do you believe?'

I nodded in response, and said something about faith being difficult, but nevertheless worth it. The conversation proceeded more slowly, and more significantly, than before. Presently the signpost to Sidmouth appeared round the bend, and it was time to drop my passengers. I never knew their names, I can scarcely recall what they looked like. But in thinking through the themes of this book, that simple question has softly echoed and re-echoed in my mind.

That is what this book is about: faith, in Christian terms. The word has an ambiguous usage. We can talk about 'the faith' in the sense of the biblical ideas, credal statements, doctrinal beliefs and so forth which constitute 'the Christian faith' in its various versions. *The* faith, in this sense, means *what* you believe. This book, however, is about *believing* – the faith *by which* you believe. Put crudely, it is about 'what it is like' to have faith. In other words, it focusses on the subjective aspect of Christian belief, rather than the objective aspect. Not that the two aspects can ever be completely separated, as we shall see. The *how* of believing is significantly shaped by *what* is believed, and can never be wholly understood apart from it. In turn, the *what* of faith includes the *how*.

'I believe in God.' What do I mean by this statement, especially the first three words? What am I saying about myself when these words pass my lips, whether in casual conversation or in the solemn utterance of the creed in a liturgical service? Just what am I doing, and what is happening to me, through this admission? Such questions can be explored from a number of angles. In particular, in current debate they are being examined as an area in the philosophy of religion, and above all in recent years this discipline has been interested in the *cognitive* aspects of faith; that is, the question as to what kind of 'knowing' of God is claimed for faith, and the relation of such knowing to the forms of knowledge in other branches of human understanding.[2] The danger here is that the study of faith is all too readily subsumed as a branch of epistemology, the science of knowledge. The question of what we can know, and how we can know it, is a crucial one throughout philosophy and theology. But if it is allowed sole rights in the study of any aspect of human experience, then distortion of the subject-matter will result. Philosophical discussion of the nature of faith, seen primarily as a problem of 'knowing', has all too often assumed, or resulted in, an over-intellectualized view of faith – and hence a drastically reduced view, since the intellect is but one aspect of being human, whereas faith indicates a direction for the whole of our existence as persons.

It is my purpose instead to try to see faith in its wholeness, not only in its intellectual aspects (which are important) but in its basic movement involving the very core of the human self as a feeling, willing, active person, a person who exists in relationship with other persons and with the world. '*Cogito, ergo sum:* I think, therefore I am', said Descartes, followed by European rationalism at large. Still timely is the warning given by that eccentric prophet of the imagination Johann Georg Hamann who inveighed against the 'unreasonable' claims of 'reason': 'Do not forget the noble *sum* on account of the *cogito*'.[3] Faith is more than a matter of mental comprehension, even comprehension of God. It is a movement of the whole person.

To understand more of the whole movement of faith, it is

necessary to have some account of faith from the inside, that is, faith trying to explain itself in its own terms. The philosopher of religion, as philosopher, must to some extent take a neutral position outside the commitment of faith itself, in examining the nature of the truth-claims of religious experience, or the nature of religious language, and their relation to other fields of enquiry. Philosophy of religion serves to remind the theologian who has a faith-commitment, and who regards his theological work as an expression of that commitment, that all faith and all theology have a context of wider religious and secular thought, which cannot be ignored if it is claimed that faith is in any way 'significant' for contemporary life and thought. At the same time, the context is not all. Faith must certainly enter into discussion with philosophy, yet if the dialogue is to have any substance faith must be true to its own peculiar nature, and be aware of its own specific stance. That may create problems for the philosopher, but this should not by itself inhibit faith's full self-presentation. Faith has its own integrity to maintain, its own course to pursue. The philosopher is more than welcome to raise questions which expose ambiguities, deflate pretensions, recognize some so-called paradoxes as contradictions, and illuminate the workings of religious language. But in the end analysis can only be an outrider of the life which it observes. Faith's prime business is to live in accordance with its own reality, to be true to its own specific nature, and, in order that this integrity may develop, to be aware of what in fact its own identity is. That has been the perennial task of Christianity, and always will be.

For Christianity *is* preeminently faith. The word 'faith' quickly became so centrally and deeply embedded in Christian parlance as to become a shorthand substitute for 'Christian faith' or 'Christian religion'. Within the pages of the New Testament itself it can be seen how soon 'believer' became the accepted technical word for 'Christian', and 'faith' for 'Christianity'. We read in Acts 2.44: 'And all who believed were together and had all things in common.' 'All who believed' is a straightforward reference to those who 'received' Peter's preaching on the Day of Pentecost (Acts 2.41) and were baptized. In Acts 5.14 there occurs another form of the Greek verb 'to believe' which in this case (*pisteuontes*) might somewhat clumsily be rendered as 'those who believed', but is generally simply translated as 'believers': 'And more than ever believers were added to the Lord.' This is but one instance where the particle of the verb 'to believe' is being used almost unconsciously as a verbal noun, meaning 'believing ones' or 'believers', describing those who have responded to the apostles' message and entered the church. So it would appear that well before receiving the title 'Christians' at Antioch and elsewhere (Acts 11.26), it was as *those who believe* that followers of the apostles identified themselves. Implicit all along, of course, is that it is the specific message concerning Jesus, crucified and risen, that is believed. This process of identification was further crystallized by the use of the word *pistos*, widely used in ordinary Greek as an adjective meaning 'faithful', but taken up in the New Testament virtually as a noun – 'faithful one', 'believing one', 'believer'. So we read in Acts 10.45: 'And the believers (*pistoi*) from among the circumcized who came with Peter were amazed, because the gift of the Holy Spirit had been poured out even on the Gentiles.' Timothy's mother is likewise described as a 'believer' (Acts 16.1) with this word. Closely parallel to this development is the New Testament usage of 'the faith' as the summary term for all that would in later ages be termed 'Christianity' (see Acts 6.7; Gal. 1.23; Phil. 1.25; Jude 3, 20; I Tim. 4.1, 6; 5.8; Titus 1.13). That the early Christians as a matter of course chose the word 'faith' to refer to the whole of the ordering of their new existence in Christ, and that to become and to be a Christian was termed 'to believe', and that the community of the church could be described as the 'household of faith' (Gal. 6.10) – all this underlines the importance of a grasp of the nature of faith for an understanding of what apostolic Christianity is about. Faith is so basic to this Christianity, because the initiative for the creation of this new existence lies in a message, the 'good news'. This message, concerning what God has done in the life, death and resurrection of Jesus Christ, is not an abstract or speculative idea to which one can respond with a casual nod or shake of the head. It is a message which includes a summons, a deeply personal demand for a change in the hearer's whole existence, and an offer of the grace by which alone that change can be made. Christianity can be summed up as faith, because Christianity is response to this message, a message which asks to be accepted in utter trust and commitment, and acted upon. 'Believe in the Lord Jesus, and you will be saved' (Acts 16.32).

If Islam means 'submission', and if for Buddhism the key-word is 'enlightenment', for Christianity the corresponding central term is faith, which certainly carries a note of submission, and also brings a certain kind of enlightenment. But in its essence faith has a way of its own. Of course Christianity is not *only* faith. 'So faith, hope, love abide, these three; but the greatest of these is love' (I Cor. 13.13). But, while knowing that they are called to exhibit love, Christians have never dared call themselves lovers. It was enough to be called *beloved* (I John 2.7; 4.7). So too with hope, the importance of which for Christianity has been emphasized so effectively in recent years by Jürgen Moltmann, Wolfhart Pannenberg and others.[4] The link between faith and hope is extremely close, and for precisely that reason they cannot be played off against each other. Hope is faith orientated towards the future, a faith in the promises; and faith is itself a grasp of the foretaste of what is promised, in the present. But, again, while Christians live by hope, they have not actually called themselves hopers, but believers.

The fact that Christian existence was initially identified as *believing* existence means that Christianity must continually examine its credentials against the criterion of faith. That is, it must repeatedly be asked whether faith is being allowed to be faith, or whether in practice it is being confused with other things, or being buried under a mass of other concerns of varying importance. The question is just as urgent at the present moment in the life of the church as at any previous time in its history, and for the rest of this chapter I would like to specify the reasons why a renewed appreciation of the nature of faith is vital for contemporary Christianity.

It is, first, a basic issue of *Christian identity*. To be a Christian is to have faith in God as known in Jesus Christ. Yet in contemporary Christian life there are all too many signs of uncertainty and confusion as to what faith means. By many, both adherents of the churches and others, Christian existence is seen almost wholly in moral terms, and often a superficial, simplistic moralism at that, relating only to a narrowly defined area of personal behaviour. I am not simply referring to the strident voice and largely prohibitive attitudes of a movement like the Festival of Light, whose day in any case seems to have come and gone. For there is a wider and more pervasive assumption, almost amounting to a folk-

religion, that Christianity is primarily a set of rules about decent
behaviour and a minimum of religious observance. The avoidance
of adultery and of covetousness then become the two greatest commandments – the former because of its explicitness, undergirded
as it is by the legal basis of marriage, the latter because of its
diffuseness which enables practically everyone apart from oneself
to be accused of greed, and thus the source of all ills in an infla-
tionary economic order is diagnosed. Of course, moral effort and
discipline as such are not to be scorned, whether in naive or highly
discriminating forms. Christianity does have a highly significant
ethical emphasis. But it is not ethics pure and simple. It is faith,
faith which gives birth to an ethical passion of its own. But faith
cannot be described simply in ethical terms, and certainly not in a
binding code of rules.

In another direction, faith is confused with a certain intellectual
understanding. Certainly, as we shall see later, Christian faith is
always a faith which seeks to understand. But only at the cost of
denying its innermost quality of personal relationship to God in
Christ, can it be confused with the absolute acceptance of certain
propositions about God, whether the highly refined concepts of a
sophisticated theology, or the unexamined slogans, culled arbitrarily from the Bible or later tradition, which masquerade as the
'true gospel' or even the 'simple gospel'. The first few generations
of Christians fought a long and sometimes confused battle against
the pretensions of so-called gnosticism, a pervasive movement in
the religious underground of the Hellenistic world, which offered
salvation to the soul on the acquisition of a certain secret 'knowledge' (*gnosis*) concerning the unseen world of demons, angels,
heaven and God. On this view, mere faith was not enough –
certainly not faith in the Jesus who had appeared in history. For
this Jesus had only the *appearance* of a man. God had not actually
come in the flesh, for material and bodily life were essentially evil.
He had only appeared human, in the guise of a man. The fullest
knowledge of the Redeemer God came only to those initiated into
the esoteric knowledge possessed by the secret cult. In contrast,
the Fourth Gospel and the Letters of John in the New Testament
emphasize that it is *faith*, personal acceptance of the bodily, human
historical Jesus as the Word made flesh, by which eternal life is
received. Even before this, the apostle Paul had flaunted the
claims of faith in the message of Christ, in the face of any demand

by which human wisdom might desire intellectual certainty about
God, independently of faith: 'For Jews demand signs and Greeks
seek wisdom, but we preach Christ crucified, a stumbling block to
Jews and folly to gentiles' (I Cor. 1.22–24).

Something parallel to that struggle is still required today.
Various brands of Christianity try to divert faith into an alien
gnosis, a man-made wisdom, varying from the avowedly funda-
mentalist to the boldly liberal, detached from actual encounter
with the living God, and which fears or despises the trusting
venture of faith. The wisdom may take the form of an apparent
allegiance to the Bible, or to the dogmatic pronouncements of
ecclesiastical authority, or to the latest 'new' theology which
finally unlocks all mysteries. All, alike, are attempts to resist the
demand for personal, trustful response to the God who has taken
the risk of coming in history as a crucified man, and who is
'known' only as each person takes the corresponding risk of
entrusting his or her life to him in return.

Regrettably, there are all too many signs in contemporary
Christianity of a recrudescent dogmatism. I write this paragraph
on the very day on which it is announced that Hans Küng has
been deprived of his official status as a teacher of the Roman
Catholic Church. The irony is that while his dismissal has been
made in the interests of a 'defence of the faith', it is Küng who
more than any other living theologian, Catholic or Protestant, has
written with such exemplary clarity on the heart of Christian
existence as faith in the justifying and sanctifying grace of God.
But Protestants are in no position to cast stones. On a popular
level at least, parallel dangers are evident within their own ranks.
The uncertainties of living in a time of rapid social and cultural
change, bringing what appears to be the endless relativization of
so many values once assumed to be of enduring worth, is induc-
ing an understandable desire for the stability offered by a return to
'traditional belief'. This would not in itself be cause for concern,
were it not that all too often it is the *phraseology* of traditional belief
that is being reiterated, parrot-fashion, almost like verbal amulets,
rather than the venture of personal faith and commitment indicated by those formulae. Against all this, of course, must be set
the more positive signs of a renewed interest in spirituality and
new forms of Christian community. But this simply means that
we are in for some lively debate in the next few years as to just

what constitutes the essence of Christianity, between those who see it in terms of adherence to verbal formulae and loyalty to institutions, and those who see it in terms of spiritual experience and actual life. In all the clamour, the claim of faith must be heard if the true identity of Christian existence is to be upheld.

A real understanding of faith is also necessary for responsible *Christian witness*. The British churches have been making considered attempts at evangelism on a broader ecumenical front than ever before. Whatever forms this may take, it involves an invitation to believe the gospel and accept its implications for every aspect of life. An invitation to believe: just what does this involve? What are people being asked to do with themselves in 'believing'? Does it involve some strenuous effort of intellectual will, in accepting what seems rationally to be highly improbable, 'as if it were true'? Does it mean a blind submission to biblical or ecclesiastical authority? Does it involve a claim to have had some odd, 'miraculous' experience which will certify the act of belief? Does it mean first being persuaded by an argument of compelling logic as to the truth of Christianity? Or what? Presentation of the gospel tends to swing between two extremes. On the one hand, there has been the high-powered authoritarian approach which softens up the individual's resistance with an emotional *Blitzkrieg* and then offers a neat package of 'gospel' as a way out of the trauma thus created. On the other hand, there has been the over-intellectualized approach of much apologetic writing, which assumes that the *main* obstacle to acceptance of the Christian message is essentially intellectual, so that if the 'image' of God or the traditional formulation of the person of Christ is made more plausible, this in itself will induce people to believe. Neither approach has any real regard for faith as a response of the whole person, and both of them demand and offer too little.

In considering the nature of *Christian action*, faith must likewise be kept fully in view. Christian action is action undertaken in faith: 'Whatever does not proceed from faith is sin' (Rom. 15.23). When this basic truth is forgotten, either of two results may follow. In some cases, Christians become paralysed by fear – fear of taking the *wrong* action, fear of failure, fear of suffering the consequences of coming out into the open and maybe taking sides in some of the most agonizing human issues in the world today. In the West, the reaction of many Christians to the rel-

atively small-scale activities of the World Council of Churches'
Programme to Combat Racism is less the result of a considered
appraisal of the pros and cons, than a knee-jerk at the suggestion
that Christian commitment may mean commitment *to* social
change rather than commitment *within* a situation of change.
Action involves taking risks, being willing to move out from
where we are safe to where so many unknown factors come into
play. Shall I go and see how they are getting on next door, and
whether they need any help? The door might be shut in my face.
I shall only find out by going. So often we cannot act, but are
helplessly bound to endless discussion and airing of platitudes
because we do not really *believe*, that is, we dare not accept that
our ultimate security is not bound up with the success or failure
of what we do, nor even its rightness or wrongness as we see it,
but in God who sustains us in all things. We dare not let go of
ourselves or give ourselves, because we do not really believe there
is anything or Anyone outside us to keep us if we fall. 'The steps
of a man are from the Lord, and he establishes him in whose way
he delights; though he fall, he shall not be cast headlong, for the
Lord is the stay of his hand' (Ps. 37.23f.).

The other possible result of a misunderstanding of faith in
relation to action, is an equally tragic activism. The underlying
motive here is that of proving, to ourselves as to others, that we
are worth something – perhaps even worthy of the title
'Christians'. We must produce results, whether in the numbers of
conversions and church attendances, or the amounts of money
raised for good causes, or whatever. There is so much wrong in
the world, there are so many problems to be solved. Life becomes
a feverish treadmill of movements to be supported, committees
to be sat on and protests to be made. One cause after another is
taken up, then dropped, as yet another appears over the horizon
and our diaries fall to pieces through over-use. The end is exhaus-
tion and disillusion. We become cynical with the world, and
maybe with ourselves. We have been so busy, that we have forgotten to ask why we are doing it at all. We have rightly despised
faith without works as a dead thing, but have assumed that so
long as we were working, we had faith. Assuming that by our
own effort and energy and insight we could change the world, we
found that the world was stronger than us. Had we understood
what is meant by the faith which overcomes the world, we would

maybe have done less, survived longer, and seen more actually achieved.

In short, it is faith which both frees us for action, and frees us from the need to be endlessly active. Therefore faith must be understood. Faith is what becoming and being a Christian are all about. That is the justification for what follows in this book.

Before concluding this chapter, however, a serious objection to the whole theme of this book must be faced. Briefly, it is that faith, taken in itself, is not a proper theme for Christian theology. All truly Christian thought is directed towards God and to his self-revelation in Christ, whereas faith is but the human response to this. Therefore to take faith seriously means taking ourselves seriously – at the expense of taking God less seriously than is his due. Behind this objection lies the formidable figure of Karl Barth, who described faith as literally, 'the last thing'[5] with which Christian theology should trouble itself. It was not, says Barth, 'a good time . . . when Christians grew eloquent over their action, over the uplift and emotion of the experience of this thing, which took place in man and when they became speechless as to *what* we may believe'.[6] Barth is referring to the tendencies in Protestant theology during the later nineteenth century, when interest centred increasingly on the subjective aspect of religion, on man's inner experiences, and less attention was paid to the reality and majesty of God himself. Barth's great achievement for twentieth-century theology was to divert it back towards God, to his majesty and grace, to his self-revelation in Christ, as the solid ground of faith. Barth's constant fear was that Christians might revert to being more interested in themselves, in their faith and 'religious experience', than in the actuality of the God in whom their faith is placed. The danger must be heeded. But precisely for the reasons given earlier, a proper examination of what faith is must be considered a part of responsible Christian thought so long as there are people who say 'I believe in God'. For all his reluctance, even Barth himself was compelled to devote *some* space to the subject of faith, whether in his exposition of the Apostles' Creed, or in a relatively few pages of his massive *Church Dogmatics*.

It must in fact be said that while an interest in faith must not be allowed to supplant a more ultimate concern with the reality of God, a true understanding of God will be impossible without an understanding of faith, if it is by faith alone that we know God. For if God is one who has, so to speak, put himself at risk by giving himself to be grasped by faith, the nature of faith is part of our understanding of God, and not simply an extra to our knowledge of him. Faith is a legitimate and important question.

2

Faith as Human

I have spoken of faith as the key-word which summarizes Christianity and provides Christians with their identity. But I have not yet said what I actually mean by faith. In the Bible itself, there is in fact only one formal definition of faith: 'Now faith is the assurance of things hoped for, the conviction of things not seen' (Heb. 11.1). Scholars have long argued over the precise meanings of the Greek words translated here by 'assurance' (*hypostasis*) and 'conviction' (*elenchos*). But both terms appear to refer to the believer's subjective attitude to the things hoped for and the things not seen, as distinct from a quality in those things themselves. The attitude is one of conviction, firm trust, assurance, certainty. For this unknown but eloquent writer to the Hebrews, faith means being sure that certain things which have not yet happened *will* happen, and that certain things invisible to the eye of sense are nevertheless real and to be reckoned with. It can be seen how in the first part of his definition the writer relates faith extremely closely to hope. Some have suggested that here the writer was reflecting the Hebraic interest in history, which underlies the Old Testament pattern of prophetic promise and fulfilment in time, whereas in the second part he was addressing his remarks more specifically to those with a Greek metaphysical interest in the distinction between the visible material world, and the spiritual, eternal realm. Be that as it may, his general sense is clear. In any case he is more concerned with faith as actually lived than with its precise analysis, as is clear from the rest of the chapter, that great panegyric on the heroes and heroines of faith down the ages, from Abel to Jesus himself 'the pioneer and perfecter of our faith'.

Now this definition of faith must obviously be understood within its context of faith in God. But it is interesting that the verse can still make a certain amount of sense if taken on its own, without any specifically 'religious' significance being read into it. It can be read as a statement about a feature of human life which is not confined to Christian or indeed any religious experience. The word 'faith', while it has come to be associated with religious experience, and most especially with Christianity, is not an exclusively religious or theological term. It commonly denotes an attitude to other people and things on a secular level. 'I've great faith in my doctor.' 'I've no faith in the British weather.' It means an attitude of trusting reliance on some person or thing other than ourselves. Further, faith in this general sense can be seen as 'the assurance of things hoped for, the conviction of things not seen'. This may not be in quite the full sense found in the specifically theological usage, but neither is it totally unconnected or dissimilar. John Macquarrie has argued that hope is as widespread a phenomenon as humanity itself, and that specifically Christian hope can be seen as the most basic and absolute form of human hope, indeed the basis and fulfilment of all so-called ordinary human hope.[1] The same is true of faith, closely related as it is to hope. The 'assurance of things hoped for' is part and parcel of everyday human life. We live in *expectation*, as people conscious not just of the present moment, but of the rest of the day, the next week, the next year, and the rest of our lives. We can live purposefully only as we have a *trusting* expectation. In part, such assurance may simply be an almost unthinking assumption in which we take for granted that things will go on as they are doing. At this moment of writing, it has just gone five o'clock. Already, I am estimating how much more of this chapter I can write before getting up and starting to lay the table for tea. My expectation is built out of past experience, of the well-grooved routine of the home in which I live. This may sound too commonplace for words, but it is just one illustration of how some kind of assurance of things still to come is integral to our conscious lives.

The same applies to 'the conviction of things not seen'. Constantly, we make acts of 'faith' in relation to what cannot yet be grasped by direct observation or tested by rational 'proof'. This is particularly so in our relations with other persons. My friend's goodwill towards me is something I trust in deeply. My trust in it is not just a fancy on my part. It is based on shared experiences, on evidences of his friendship, help, understanding and so on. But, that he can be completely relied upon to be my friend requires my continued trust. He could, conceivably, be a very clever actor, simply pretending to be my friend and cynically exploiting my trust for some ulterior motive. After all, the deepest motives of people are always in a measure hidden from us. That we continue to find strength and fulfilment in each other's company largely derives from the trust we place in each other. Were I to lose my trust, I would soon lose my friend.

In short, some sort of 'faith' plays an essential part in a recognizably human life. By faith is meant *living in conscious reliance on the consistency of some reality other than ourselves, and on which some aspect of our good depends.* Where the 'reality' other than ourselves is God, the fact that he is the ultimate reality transcending all finite realities gives faith in him a specific quality of its own. But it still falls within the general definition of faith just given.

It is important that this should be recognized both by Christian believers, and by sceptics. The latter are prone to feel that faith in God is necessarily some freakish, well-nigh pathological condition of the human psyche. Or that faith involves some mental acrobatics, as in the oft-quoted schoolboy definition of faith as 'believing what you know isn't true'. Or that it means some blind submission to authority, in which one surrenders one's own integrity. Or, quite simply, that faith is a second-best option to cope with the uncertainty and ambivalence of our understanding of ultimate issues. The presupposition of this view is that real certainty comes by direct observation and logical deduction therefrom. The scientific method, basing itself solely upon empirical data and experimental verification, is the prime path to knowledge today, whereas faith means resorting to sheer acceptance of ideas in the absence of proofs ·by rational means, or even in the face of disproof by such means.

However, the scope of this kind of 'rationality' is extremely limited when one takes into account how we actually live as active, feeling, relating human beings. Or rather, putting it more positively, we should say that faith, in the sense of the general definition given above, is an ingredient in practically every field of conscious human endeavour and responsibility. In order to live freely and purposefully, we need to act trustingly in relation to other persons and entities in our environment. Like the air we breathe, it is such an essential yet commonplace element in our existence that we barely notice its importance until we are deprived of it, as can happen in certain forms of mental disorder. Normally, most of us do not worry whether the ground might suddenly open under our feet, or whether the ice-caps might suddenly melt and flood the continents, or whether other people are continually spying on us and 'out to get us'. Yet some people do have obsessional anxieties of this kind, and as anyone who has tried to be of help to such people knows, rational argument is useless to counter such fears. Indeed, on strictly logical grounds, how can we be certain that such disasters will *not* occur at any moment? The 'normal' or healthy attitude requires an implicit trust in the continued, consistent behaviour of the natural world and other people. This may well seem to be an extremely attenuated form of 'trust', almost an unthinking assumption. But whatever we call it, it is evident that ordinary life in the world requires an *expectation* of the reliability and consistency of the environment in which we live: an expectation which can be confirmed when our expectations are actually met, but which cannot be 'proved' absolutely in advance.

It is therefore worth reflecting briefly on almost any of the varied activities that are involved in a purposeful and creative human life, in order to see just how basic is faith, as a trusting reliance upon what is not ourselves. I have already referred to friendship, and to the basic sense that our natural environment is on the whole 'safe'. One could also refer to the immense place that *learning* occupies in human life, from the first basic bodily functions acquired in infancy, through the more complex mental and social techniques learned through childhood, to the demands which work and adult responsibilities bring for acquiring new skills, and to the new techniques and disciplines necessary for adjustment to old age. Man is a continually learning animal. It has often been pointed out, especially in academic and vocational training, how important *motivation* is for effective learning. It is the pupil or student who *wants* to learn who is most likely to learn. But such motivation is an expression of, and grounded in, a deep sense of *trust* at several levels: trust in the basic worthwhileness of what is being learnt, and trust in the competence and commitment of the one who is teaching it. Where this trust breaks down, as when a student (rightly or wrongly) feels that part of the curriculum is quite irrelevant to his future career, or (rightly or wrongly) that the teacher does not know his subject, so does the learning process. Learning is one of the best examples of human trust at work, since it requires that we acknowledge ourselves as reliant upon a world of ideas, skills and experiences which are not yet our own, but which may become ours through attention and application to them.

Learning, as educationists often point out, is most effective when the learner somehow discovers for himself the truth which is being disclosed to him, as distinct from simply accepting it on the blind authority of the teacher. The good teacher enables the pupils to see the truth for themselves, and grasp it for themselves. Often, illumination comes not just by noting a fact that we have not known before, but in grasping an insight which proves significant through its capacity to open up a whole new area of understanding. The young child, struggling with long division sums, jumps with relief and delight when he 'gets it right', not just because he has got that particular sum right, but because he now senses that by the same method he can do all such sums that may come his way. Discovery, whether on this elementary level, or in the higher reaches of intellectual research, involves coming upon an insight which is seen as significant precisely because it opens up so many more possibilities of knowledge and understanding. That it will do so, is in part at least a matter of trust – not blind trust, or an arbitrary assertion of opinion, but an intuitive projection from what has been seen, to what is not yet fully and directly seen.

Indeed, it has become almost commonplace to point out that progress in the natural sciences, for instance, in practice by no means always comes simply by what is popularly known as the 'scientific method' – the collection of facts, the summary of data, the construction of a hypothesis to account for those data, and then the testing of that hypothesis by controlled experiments and further observations. Imagination and insight are also involved all along the way, most especially in the framing of a hypothesis. Michael Polanyi has stressed the personal and passionate elements in the scientific search for truth, and identifies certain of the qualities which are less obvious, but vital, in a theory which points us towards 'objective' or 'rational' truth about the universe. He writes:

Comprehension is neither an arbitrary act nor a passive experience, but a responsible act claiming universal validity. Such knowing is indeed *objective* in the sense of establishing contact with a hidden reality; a contact that is defined as the condition for anticipating an indeterminate range of yet unknown (and perhaps yet inconceivable) true implications.[2]

Again, concerning a theory regarded as 'rational':

We accept it in the hope of making contact with reality; so that, being really true, our theory may yet show forth its truth through future centuries in ways undreamt of by its authors.[3]

Polanyi is pointing out that even intellectual understanding is more than a cold, dispassionate discernment of the correspondence between a theory and 'things as they actually are'. It is, rather, an excited, hopeful, expectant – and I would say *trusting* – vision of the power of an idea to unlock and reveal things as yet baffling or unknown. It is indeed a form of human faith as the assurance of things hoped for, the conviction of things not (yet) seen.

It should not be surprising that certain theologians, in particular, have pointed out how deep-seated is the faith-element in human exploration of the universe, whether practically or theoretically. At bottom, it is faith in the worthwhileness of the world as an object of knowledge and understanding which undergirds the exploration, and, closely linked with this, faith in the amenability of our environment to our understanding. H. H. Farmer went so far as to suggest that 'the whole evolution of life has depended upon a fundamental optimism, or faith, in living creatures that they are adequate to their world'. He continues:

In man this fundamental optimism becomes more or less conscious of itself. Truth, he feels, is good to know; a man gains in well-being by knowing the truth; and that which in the long run is not good to know, brings with it no enhancement or enrichment, rather the reverse, cannot be, or at least is not likely to be, true. It is surely this deep-seated pragmatic conviction which lies in part behind and sustains man's restless explorations of his world, searchings for truth, constructions of unifying and interpretative systems of thought, all that enterprise which receives its most impressive expression in the activity of a great university.[4]

It is again to Farmer that we may turn for a fine definition of this 'human faith':

> Faith is the awareness of an overshadowing reality which is not perceptible to the senses, nor as yet expressible in precise terms; but which is known with certitude to be somehow the source of all that has been experienced, and the promise of all that will assuredly be even yet more fully experienced, of good in man's life.[5]

It is by faith, therefore, that we live purposeful, responsible and creative human lives, and this faith is a trust which reaches from the continuance of our daily routine and dealings with other people, to a deeper and more fundamental sense that life is meant to be worthwhile and fulfilling, that the world about us is worthy of our trust and amenable to our understanding. This is not to play down the importance of rationality, in the sense of deductive reasoning for instance. But our powers of reasoning do not function by themselves. They are set to work by, and in the interests of, our exploratory and creative urges, which exhibit trust in what the eye cannot yet see.

So too Wolfhart Pannenberg speaks of 'trust' as a fundamental aspect of human existence:

> Only trust allows the soul room to breathe. Every day men base their lives on an all-embracing trust, which may express itself as a confidence in the particular circumstances which surround me, in the reliability of the things I deal with and, not least, in the people with whom I have to do. Even the most distrustful man cannot avoid trusting. Not of course all the time. He can refuse to trust here and there, but not everywhere and at all times.[6]

In a similar fashion to Farmer, Pannenberg goes on to speak of a fundamental trust, 'a deeper and unconditional trust' which remains 'the basic condition for the formation of a healthy personality'.

In normal circumstances most people probably do not think much about the real basis of the trust which sustains their lives. We often only become conscious of what it is when the mainstay of our trust is shattered, thereby endangering our very capacity for living itself.[7]

The importance of the faith-element in human existence has to do with the peculiar two-fold nature of being a person. We are, on the one hand, highly self-conscious individual selves, and on the other hand selves who cannot exist out of relationship to other selves and to the world. Being a human person involves being aware of oneself, able to 'look at oneself' or, in more philosophical language, to transcend oneself. I am not simply here, like a stone. I *know* I am here. I do not simply function, like a machine or even a higher animal. I can make conscious choices, and can reflect on those choices. What I am to be, depends in part on what I decide to be. I can 'make something' of myself. Of course, there are real limitations on my choices – limitations of my genetic inheritance, my upbringing, my social and cultural context, all that makes up my particular setting in space and time. Most crucially of all, my finitude is marked by death. Like all creatures, I shall die. But, being human, I *know* that I shall die one day, and that only sharpens my self-consciousness.

But it is not of ourselves alone that we are conscious. We are aware of an environment to which we are related and from which we simply cannot abstract ourselves. Vital to being a mature person is the ability to distinguish between oneself and one's surroundings, while at the same time making the relationship which has to exist between them. This is a process of great length and complexity, beginning in earliest infancy and possibly, for many of us, never wholly realized. The infant only gradually learns to distinguish himself from the environment which is his mother, and to tell the difference between his body and hers. Gradually he recognizes the hand that plays over his face as his own, part of himself, as distinct from the rattle which he can hold but which is part of the world outside himself. Step by step, a distance between oneself and the world is realized, and at the same time the world – or parts of it – is known as capable of being 'held'. Crucial to this growth is the reliable love of the mother who provides warmth and security as well as nourishment, enabling the potentially awesome awareness of being a distinct centre of consciousness to be borne without the child succumbing to the dread of being lost and annihilated in face of what is not himself. However much this journey to self-consciousness and world-consciousness may be imperfectly understood, it seems that its early stages are vital to the formation of a personality who can cope with responsibilities and relationships in later life. Parental warmth, acceptance and reliability mediate to the child the sense that the environment is basically trustworthy, that other people are worthy of trust and affection, and that the child's own ventures of trust and affection towards other people, and explorations of his world, will on the whole prove rewarding to him.

If we are to live securely and creatively, we need to respect the 'otherness' of what is outside us, and we need a sense of our own worth in this environment of 'otherness'. Those who have little sense of 'otherness' treat people and things simply as extensions of themselves, as objects for their own use. They wreak havoc around them, and eventually for themselves too. That is the seedbed of dictatorship, on whatever scale. On the other hand, those who are all too conscious of the limitless realm of persons and things about them, with too little sense of their own worth and selfhood, live in constant dread of all 'otherness', and cannot make effective and lasting relationships. Their life is one of anxiety and continual retreat from commitment, from job to job, from pastime to pastime, from lover to lover, always looking for the final, safe corner.

The way to personal maturity lies through avoiding such views of existence as an either-or battle between oneself and what is other than oneself. Maturity comes through perceiving the reality in distinction of ourselves and our environment, and the possibilities of a positive relationship between them. This requires, on the one hand, that we allow our environment to be itself, and other people to be themselves. On the other hand, it requires that we offer ourselves as persons who have a contribution to make to our world and other people through exploration, understanding and appreciation. The connection, in short, has to be a relationship of trust, a movement outward in acceptance and commitment. 'All real living is meeting' in Martin Buber's famous phrase – and Buber meant not simply the I-Thou relationships between persons, but also the I-Thou relationships which in a mysterious way can even exist in encounters between ourselves and inanimate beings. The need for trust is thus built into the very fabric of our nature as conscious persons who live in an environment which requires our participation and interaction if our lives are to have any meaning and purpose. We cannot give purpose to our lives, or find any fulfilment, by dwelling on ourselves in isolation. Narcissus dies through contemplating himself.

The argument of this chapter is not, in itself, an attempt to justify faith in the religious or specifically Christian sense of faith in God. One cannot argue from the deep and widespread fact of faith as a human phenomenon to the reasonableness of believing in *God*. But faith in God, given the context of human existence as one which requires faith at so many levels, is not to be dismissed on account of its being *faith*, as though faith were in principle a poor substitute for 'rational proof' or 'demonstration' or 'certain knowledge' (as in direct sensory perception or mathematical logic). For it is through faith that reality outside ourselves becomes accessible to us, enabling both our acting and understanding as persons. One may even go as far as J. G. Hamann in saying 'Our own being and the existence of all things outside us must be believed, and cannot be established in any other way'.[8]

Faith, as I have defined it, is a trusting reliance upon some reality other than ourselves – trust not simply in the mere existence of that reality, but in its 'worthwhileness' for our good. 'Faith' and 'belief' are commonly used almost interchangeably. But 'belief' denotes a more intellectualized attitude, implying assent to some statement claiming truth. I believe that there is a country called Australia, although I have never been there. Faith moves beyond this attitude of credence in geographical statements, into a situation of trust which acknowledges that I have some personal stake in what is believed. If I were actually booking a flight to Australia, my belief would be moving into such trust, for I would be venturing my life on the reality of Australia's existence.

The Christian claim is that the reality of our environment is not simply one of space and time, or what may broadly be described as 'nature'. The spatio-temporal world is real – that is a view for which Christianity has repeatedly had to fight from its earliest days, against those who would devalue matter, time and history in the interests of positing a timeless, eternal and wholly spiritual realm as alone truly real. But, in Christian faith, in and through the spatio-temporal world we become aware that this is not the sum total of our environment. There is a transcendent dimension, an 'otherness', which cannot be accounted for simply in terms of the world itself. Or put slightly differently, the world (including man himself) raises not only the question 'What is it?' but 'Whence does it come?' To faith, it is not grounded in itself, but in an ultimately primal reality. The world is not just there, it is given.

It is of grace. This grace is not grasped just as a theory about the givenness of the world, nor yet just an inkling derived from contemplating the goodness and beauty of the world (which in any case is extremely problematical in face of the massive facts of evil and suffering). It springs from encounter with the person and story of Jesus Christ, and the peculiar impact which he makes upon us here and now. In him, grace moves from being an inkling or an idea into an actual, transforming power in our lives. The Word becomes flesh. Through him, we are offered a vision of what our environment ultimately is: self-giving, gracious love which sustains us and all that is in being, and which is ceaselessly and unreservedly active in forming us into a humanity which reflects the same loving nature. Faith in God is the ultimate human faith, for it is faith in the most fundamental reality other than ourselves. Like all reality other than ourselves, God requires faith in order to be known.

I have then argued for a considerable degree of continuity between the nature of faith in God, and 'faith as human' in the wider sense. Both, alike, mean a trusting reliance upon what is not ourselves, as the only way in which that other reality can become accessible to us, and whereby we can enter into fruitful relationship to it. Of course much more needs to be said about the differences. God, being transcendent and 'other' to us in a way uniquely different from anything in the spatio-temporal world, can never become comprehensible to us in the way things in the world become amenable to our minds. What is more, some Christians may object that for all the similarities and analogies between 'ordinary' human trust and faith in God, the latter is absolutely and qualitatively different since it is a supernatural gift of God himself. He gives and creates our faith in him, as a work of sheer grace. This is an important element in orthodox Christian theology, and I shall have more to say about it in later chapters. Here, it can simply be remarked that even so-called 'ordinary' human faith is not quite such a straightforward matter as may first appear. In its fullness, the trust of a person in a reality other than himself cannot be wholly described as his own act, as though it were purely self-determined. For it is a *response* to the other reality, and is in a measure *evoked* by that other reality. This is certainly the case in relationships between persons. I do not just decide to trust someone with whom I am becoming a friend, either arbitrarily or calculatingly. In a real if indefinable way my trust is drawn out of me by him, and owes at least as much to his approach to me as mine to him. Something of the sort is true also of our attitudes to non-personal realities. We speak, for example, of the 'appeal' which scenery, or music, makes to us; or of the way in which the molecular structure of living cells 'fascinates' us. Such language, verging on the poetic (and romantic poetry at that), may receive terse treatment from commonsense linguistic philosophers. But the very fact that we use it so often, and without alarm, indicates that over wide areas our human existence is existence in relationship, of mutual reciprocity between ourselves and what is not ourselves. In no area do we live purely out of ourselves. We are enabled to live through trusting relationships with what is 'other', and even the trust itself comes as a gift.

3

Faith as Trust

I have already described faith as a trustful reliance upon the consistency and good of some reality other than ourselves. Christian faith is such a trustful relationship with the reality of God, the ultimate environing reality of our lives, as seen supremely in the person of Jesus Christ. Here, where we begin to explore the nature of specifically Christian faith, this chapter will be devoted to underlining the fact that this faith is primarily and basically *personal trust*. No apology is offered for speaking simply, even naively, here. Other things need to be said, and will be said later, about faith and its relationship to intellectual understanding, credal statements, activity in good works, and so on. But all too often, both by sophisticated theologians and so-called simple believers, this primary feature of Christian faith is ignored. Faith is confused with accepting as authoritative certain statements, perhaps those of the classic creeds of the church, or those which claim to summarize the essential teaching of the Bible about salvation or the divinity of Christ, or even those which bind one to a certain view of the Bible itself (such as its verbal inspiration or infallibility). Such views of faith, all in their different ways, put an intellectualistic straitjacket on faith. Or, faith may be confused with the claim to have had certain types of spiritual experience. Or, with the will-power to be active in some cause or other, whether evangelism or social service or political reform. None of these are irrelevant to faith, but they must not be confused with its heart.

Faith is personal trust in the gracious God known in Jesus. It is reliance upon the God who moves in love towards us. Faith is thus very simple in its essence. Yet how hard it is to be simple and stay simple!

The person who has faith relies totally and unreservedly upon God as the sustaining power and security of his or her life. We saw in the last chapter that a feature of human life is that as individual persons we are conscious of a certain 'apartness' of ourselves from other persons and our environment, and that equally we can only live in relationship with other persons and things. A consequence of this is that a big question-mark is placed against each one of us, as to our identity. That I am is one thing. *Who* I am, and who I am meant to be, are quite other matters. I can get only a short distance in trying to answer 'Who?', if I restrict my enquiry to examining myself and my own opinions about myself. I know my name – but even that was given me by my parents. I have my store of memories and experiences which are my record of my life-story so far, yet most of this story involves my interactions with other people; and their attitudes to me – of acceptance, rebuke, encouragement, love, fear and so on – deeply affect my view of myself. I am aware of the various roles I play as son, husband, father, friend, minister, teacher and the like. But the very word 'role' indicates that I am but an actor in a life-drama far bigger than myself, and my part has meaning only as it is set in that bigger script. So to a great extent the question of who I am is answerable only in terms of *to whom* I am such a person. I cannot wholly decide or determine my identity; others are needed to define it and accept it.

Of course, to a degree it is my responsibility to choose and shape an identity for myself. I am not simply a piece of clay to be moulded by others' expectations. And one of the great human struggles in the world today concerns those categories of people who are becoming aware that hitherto their identity has been stamped upon them by others, or by the wider community as a whole. To reject the stereotype that one has been conditioned to accept for oneself, whether that stereotype be racial, social or sexual, is a necessary (and often painful) step towards fuller maturity as a person. But even if we exercise some choice as to 'who' we shall be, we still seek an identity which will be recognized and accepted by others.

The question of who I am can partly be answered by what I do and achieve. Some achievements can give me satisfaction whether or not they are recognized by others. To visit a certain cathedral, or climb a particular mountain and enjoy the view from the summit, can provide a purely personal sense of enjoyment, and might indeed be all the richer for being in solitude. But if in any way I wish to 'make my mark on the world', then however greatly I measure my achievements by my own standards, I am considerably dependent on recognition by other people. This can become a chief source of anxiety underlying many of our ambitions. We think we shall have reached a lasting sense of security when we have written a book, or found a marriage partner, or been elected to a certain office. But deep down there is the nagging fear that any recognition this brings us will not last. And so we drive ourselves to do yet more. Our achievements may be real in an objective sense. We may well be utterly convinced that they deserve recognition. But the recognition by others can never be guaranteed, never automatically evoked by the achievements themselves. Indeed, one of the lessons that anyone with a modicum of awareness soon learns, is that the amount of respect and approval we receive from others seems to be in inverse proportion to the conscious efforts we make to get it. The most 'likeable' people are those who, while certainly sensitive to others' feelings, make no deliberate effort to be liked or even noticed, but cheerfully pursue their way according to their lights. We can only live in a trusting openness to whatever recognition, however much or little, comes our way.

The question of 'who' each one of us is, is also made problematic by our own deep-seated fears and anxieties about ourselves, especially as these feelings are so often manifestations of guilt. This is a profound and complex subject, whether considered from the psychological, clinical or theological aspects. Suffice it to say that many of us struggle against the fear that we are not 'acceptable' for what we are. As individuals, separate centres of consciousness who nevertheless can only live in relationships with others, we seek a sense of *belonging*: belonging to intimates in the family and one or more circles of friends, belonging to the communities of work and leisure, and to the society and culture in which we are set, and, moreover, in the total environment of the universe which is itself environed in the ultimate reality called God.

We cannot, in short, ensure our acceptance by what we do or by

how we present ourselves to others. In the end, it can only be
received as and when it is given to us. It is therefore a matter of
trust. And faith in God means an unreserved entrusting of ourselves to his graciousness towards us; a reliance upon his love for
us as the sole guarantee of our essential worth as persons, and as
the basis for our hope of becoming the persons we can be. As this
trust, faith is the means by which we receive 'salvation' – a word
with a number of levels of meaning in the biblical and Christian
tradition. On the one hand, salvation denotes 'safety', 'being made
safe', or to use the common modern term, 'security'. Those who
entrust themselves wholly to God know that they are ultimately
safe, in life and in death. They know their identity, they know
who they are, as those who belong to God and receive the bene-
fits of his loving purposes for them and for the whole world. This
sense of the security of a trusting faith in God, and the sense of
belonging which it brings, was movingly expressed by Dietrich
Bonhoeffer in his poem 'Who Am I?', written in a Nazi prison.

> Who am I? They often tell me
> I would step from my cell's confinement
> calmly, cheerfully, firmly,
> like a squire from his country-house.
>
> Who am I? They often tell me
> I would talk to my warders
> freely and friendly and clearly,
> as though it were mine to command.
>
> Who am I? They also tell me
> I would bear the days of misfortune
> equably, smilingly, proudly,
> like one accustomed to win.
>
> Am I really then all that which other men tell of?
> Or am I only what I know of myself,
> restless and longing and sick like a bird in a cage,
> struggling for breath, as though hands were compressing my
>   throat,
> yearning for colours, for flowers, for the voices of birds,
> thirsting for words of kindness, for neighbourliness,
> trembling with anger at despotisms and petty humiliation,
> tossing in expectation of great events,

powerlessly trembling for friends at an infinite distance,
weary and empty at praying, at thinking, at making,
faint, and ready to say farewell to it all?

Who am I? This or the other?
Am I one person today, and tomorrow another?
Am I both at once? A hypocrite before others,
and before myself a contemptibly woebegone weakling?
Or is something within me still like a beaten army,
fleeing in disorder from victory already achieved?

Who am I? They mock me, these questions of mine.
Whoever I am, thou knowest, O God, I am thine.[1]

Trust in God is a reliant assurance in God, trust that God is for
us, and therefore we are secure come what may – failure, pain,
disgrace, our own guilt, death. In him we are more secure than
we could ever be through our own acts and achievements, or the
status we confer on ourselves or which we try to force other
people to confer on us.

The other main nuance of salvation is that of health, wholeness,
the fullness of life that is available to us as human beings: bodily,
mentally, spiritually, in community as well as individually. Faith
as trust in God is a confident reliance upon his gracious power
which is working towards the goal of bringing us into that fullness
of life which is health indeed, an ever-deepening relationship to
God himself, to other people, and in fact to all creation.

Both main senses of salvation, of 'security' (or 'belonging') and
'health' (or 'wholeness') are conveyed in the rich and beautiful
biblical word 'peace', the Hebrew *shalom*. The apostle Paul sums up
the whole Christian understanding of the relationship between this
shalom and trustful faith when he writes: 'Therefore, since we are
justified by faith, we have peace with God through our Lord Jesus
Christ' (Rom. 5.1). Much could and should be said about the term
'justified by faith' which has played such a central, and sometimes
highly controversial, part in the story of Christianity. Basically it
derives from the lawcourt. Man stands before God as his Maker
and Judge, the One to whom man is ultimately accountable, and
to whom alone he can look for final succour. Man may consider
himself well-deserving of approval for his good deeds, or deserv-
ing of punishment for his bad deeds. But, however good or bad

he may be, considered in himself, his salvation cannot be wrought by himself, or conferred on him by himself. He can only receive it, as a gift. That is, in forensic language, he cannot 'justify' himself before God. It is God who justifies him, sinner that he is in fact or righteous man that he may be in theory. He can only trustingly rely upon what is not himself, in this case the sheer grace and goodness of God. And God *is* gracious. The peace – security and wholeness – which man seeks can only be grasped in sheer, receptive trust.

This was more than a peculiar idea of Paul's own imagination. It is consistent with the whole experience of the people of Israel as witnessed to in the Old Testament. They were a 'chosen' people, called and befriended by God not because of what they were, or what they did, but because of his gracious purpose. 'The Lord your God has chosen you to be a people for his own possession, out of all the peoples that are on the face of the earth. It was not because you were more in number than any other people that the Lord set his love upon you and chose you, for you were the fewest of all peoples; but it is because the Lord loves you, and is keeping the oath which he swore to your fathers, that the Lord has brought you out with a mighty hand, and redeemed you from the house of bondage, from the hand of Pharaoh king of Egypt' (Deut. 7.6b–8). One of the commonest popular errors is the idea that while the New Testament speaks of a God of love, the Old Testament portrays a God who is primarily a stern lawgiver and a vengeful judge. The Ten Commandments are often referred to by stern moralists, while omitting the crucial heading which introduces them: 'I am the Lord your God who brought you out of the land of Egypt, out of the house of bondage' (Deut. 5.6). God enjoins obedience on his people because he is the God who has first joined himself to them in absolute love and faithfulness. The whole story of the Old Testament is that of how God, through all the vicissitudes of the history of Israel, and despite all Israel's failures in love and loyalty to him, remains the God of Israel, ever seeking to elicit his people's response to his love, ever seeking to deepen their awareness of his covenanted grace. He is to be obeyed, because he shows himself utterly to be *trusted*.

The New Testament witness is that Jesus is the climax of the dealings of this gracious God with his people. Jesus embodies within himself God's graciousness. He preaches the good news of

God's reign, God's love and mercy. He forgives sins, and eats with sinners. He heals the sick. He feeds the hungry. He lifts up the despairing, and warns the proud. He gives himself utterly and, at the end, literally. He also embodies the true response which God desires from his people. He himself is the one who utterly trusts God and unswervingly follows the path of loyalty, despite the seductive temptations of power, status and safety, and despite the unspeakable final suffering of the cross. At the end, he apparently has nothing to show for all his ministry, no achievement, no recognition. He dies the death of one rejected and abandoned, a death which in the religious eyes of his contemporaries showed that he was 'accursed', rejected even by God. He cries the cry of the Psalmist, 'My God, my God, why have you forsaken me?' In that final darkness, there is no other way than that of utter trust. However the resurrection is to be precisely understood (if such a mystery *can* be fully understood), it is at least the testimony that God did indeed vindicate Jesus and his trust. From defeat to victory, from humiliation to exaltation, from death to life, God brought the man who uniquely taught and lived the grace of God, and who himself utterly trusted in that grace.

Faced with this Jesus as the climax and summary of all that God wishes to say to us, we can do no other than see God as the God of utter grace which is grasped in sheer glad, grateful *trust*. By this trust we indeed 'have peace with God through our Lord Jesus Christ'. He is *for us*. In face of that, all our claims to deserve his goodness are irrelevant, as are our fears that our failures put us beyond his care. It was because he saw this as the heart of the gospel that Paul fought so vehemently for the notion of 'justification by faith' – perhaps better expressed as 'justification by grace through faith' – during the first generation of Christianity. On this, he saw, depended the validity of the Christian mission to the gentiles. Did those who became Christians have to adopt Jewish rules of behaviour and religious observance? For many in the earliest churches, the issue was far from clear-cut. Jesus himself was a Jew, and had even spoken of a righteousness exceeding that of the scribes and pharisees. The mother-church in Jerusalem probably saw itself as part of Judaism, albeit the true Judaism. Paul himself vigorously refuted the charge that he was undermining the importance of moral conduct – and indeed he continued to keep certain Jewish religious customs himself. But in

Paul's eyes, if salvation is God's gift, apprehended by a trusting faith in the crucified and risen Jesus, then those who believe in this way are all of equal standing before God and in the fellowship of the church, irrespective of religious, racial or social origin. First things first. Let all apprehend God in Christ by faith, and then work out the ensuing obedience, which for all, Jew and gentile alike, will supremely be a life of love (*agape*), a mirror of the kind of love with which all have been loved by God. As far as salvation was concerned, faith as trust in God's grace was central. It could not be allowed to stand qualified or supplemented by legalistic observances.

Of Paul's writings on faith, a section of his Letter to the Galatians provides a convenient crystallization of his thought. Paul had evidently heard that the Galatian Christian community was being influenced by those seeking to impose certain Judaistic observances as necessary to salvation, in addition to faith in Christ. The third chapter opens thus:

O foolish Galatians! Who has bewitched you, before whose eyes Jesus Christ was publicly portrayed as crucified? Let me ask you only this: Did you receive the Spirit by works of the law, or by hearing with faith? Are you so foolish? Having begun with the Spirit, are you now ending with the flesh? Did you experience so many things in vain? – if it really is in vain. Does he who supplies the Spirit to you and works miracles among you do so by works of the law, or by hearing with faith? (vv. 1–5)

Here, Paul is appealing directly to the experience of the Galatian Christians. They had experienced God's power, the activity of his Spirit, in an extraordinary way. When did this begin to happen? When they began to attempt a more strenuous religious rectitude? No. It was when they simply turned in utter trust to Jesus Christ as the graciousness of God. That was the point at which the very power and blessing of God entered upon them in a new way. Notice that Paul does not state that he had at first taught them a doctrine of justification by faith. What they had been given was the picture of Jesus Christ as crucified. In face of *that*, sheer trusting reliance upon God's grace can be the only appropriate response.

Next, he pursues a differently based argument:

Thus Abraham 'believed God, and it was reckoned to him as righteousness'. So you see that it is men of faith who are the sons of Abraham. And the scripture, foreseeing that God would justify the Gentiles by faith, preached the gospel beforehand to Abraham, saying, 'In you shall all the nations be blessed'. So then, those who are men of faith are blessed with Abraham who had faith (vv. 6–9).

This is an argument from biblical history, and is particularly apt in dealing with those who argue that to become a Christian involves, in a sense, becoming a Jew in attitudes and observances. But what, Paul is asking, is the essential mark of those who claim to belong to the stock of Abraham, the father of all Israel? Quoting Genesis 15.6, Paul insists that at the very beginning of Israel's story, Abraham himself was marked only by his faith: a hopeful, reliant trust in the God who had called him and promised him descendants. This was *before* the Jewish ritual orders had been established, *before* the giving of the Law to Moses, *before* even the physical mark of circumcision was enjoined upon Abraham as symbolizing the special nature of his family. Paul follows this argument in greater detail in Romans chapter 4. It was evidently one he had to repeat a number of times, orally as well as in writing. The essence of being God's people is trust which casts itself upon God's gracious call and promises, which does not claim anything for itself but looks only to the power and love of God.

Paul then approaches the question from yet another angle.

For all who rely on works of the law are under a curse; for it is written, 'Cursed be every one who does not abide by all things written in the book of the law, and do them'. Now it is evident that no man is justified before God by the law; for 'He who through faith is righteous shall live'; but the law does not rest on faith, for 'He who does them shall live by them'. Christ redeemed us from the curse of the law, having become a curse for us – for it is written, 'Cursed be everyone who hangs on a tree' – that in Christ Jesus the blessings of Abraham might come upon the Gentiles, that we might receive the promise of the Spirit through faith (vv. 10–13).

Here, Paul is arguing as a well-trained rabbinic scholar, appealing directly neither to immediate Christian experience nor to Israel's history, but to what he sees as the essential logic of the scriptures (that is, the Old Testament, of course) in the light of Christ. On the one hand, failure to obey the whole of the Mosaic law brings judgment upon oneself – which implies that anyone who looks for salvation in this direction is condemned as hopeless. For who could claim total and absolute obedience to the law? On the other hand, an actual right standing with God ('justification') is in any case not a matter of legal rectitude. 'He who through *faith* is rightous shall live', Paul states quoting Habakkuk 2.4. It is a matter of argument whether in the original Hebrew and in the context of the prophecy itself Habakkuk meant quite the same thing by 'faith' as Paul does here and in Romans 1.17. The Old Testament meaning could well be that of 'faithfulness' or 'loyalty' to God through suffering, rather than Paul's sense of sheer trust. But Paul's argument does not stand or fall by this particular point of exegesis, for as we shall see later there is an idea of faith closely parallel to Paul's diffused throughout the Old Testament. For Paul, moreover, it is the cross of Jesus which is the literally the crux of the whole issue. Christ himself died as one accursed in his manner of execution. Yet he is the one vindicated by God, and through whom the Spirit has come to those who trust in him. Legalistic criteria are therefore irrelevant to one's standing in relation to God. Not, Paul goes on to argue in the rest of the chapter, that the law has no part in God's purposes. 'The law was our custodian until Christ came, that we might be justified by faith' (v. 24). The law does indeed reveal God's will for human behaviour. But men cannot rely on their knowledge of it, or their attempts at keeping it, or anything else of which they might 'boast' as having in themselves or doing for themselves, for their ultimate security and salvation. That, as shown in the cross of Jesus, in God's gift, grasped in trust.

Paul's writings came to occupy a central place in the church's canon of scriptures. Not that he won the battle for all time. The saving efficacy of trusting faith has continually been endangered by one form or another of religious and moral legalism. Moreover, because of the apparent complexity of his arguments and his use of such terms as 'justification', Paul's teaching has sometimes been deprecated in favour of the so-called 'simple' teaching of Jesus himself. In fact there is an exceedingly close parallel between Paul's view of faith, and the response which the teaching of Jesus sought to elicit from his hearers as recorded in the synoptic gospels. The message of Jesus' Galilean ministry is summed up as: 'The time is fulfilled, and the kingdom of God is at hand; repent, and believe in the gospel' (Mark 1.15). He preached the present, manward movement of God's mercy, and what he called for was a response of openness and acceptance of this mercy, a change of heart (repentance) marked by a trusting apprehension of God's kindness conveyed by the 'good news'. Luke records Jesus at the outset of his ministry as applying to himself the words from Isaiah: 'The Spirit of the Lord is upon me, because he has anointed me to preach good news to the poor. He has sent me to proclaim release to the captives, and recovering of sight to the blind, to set at liberty those who are oppressed, to proclaim the acceptable year of the Lord' (Luke 4.18f.). He looked for faith in this graciousness of God – not faith in an idea of it, but trust in it as an event, a reality offered to men here and now. So, he appreciated the faith of the men who brought the paralytic and lowered him through the roof on a stretcher; the faith of the centurion who begged that Jesus simply speak the word and his servant would be healed; the faith of the sick woman who touched the hem of his garment; and so on. In the gospels such trusting faith is contrasted with *fear*, such as the disciples showed in the storm on the lake (Mark 4.40), or the *anxiety* about daily needs (Matt. 6.25–34). The 'unbelief' at which Jesus 'marvels' in his home town of Nazareth is a refusal to accept the healing power of God available through his ministry (Mark 6.6). As with Paul, so with Jesus faith is a trusting apprehension of God's gracious power to hold, sustain and save. Moreover, Luke records a parable that might almost have been told by Paul. A pharisee and a tax-collector (that pariah of Jewish society) stand praying in the temple. The pharisee thanks God that he is a virtuous man as compared with the tax-collector who for his part dare not even look up, but says merely 'God, be merciful to me a sinner'. 'I tell you, this man went down to his house justified rather than the other; for every one who exalts himself will be humbled, but he who humbles himself will be exalted' (Luke 18.14). What Jesus calls 'exalting oneself' corresponds to Paul's view of 'boasting': the tendency to look to oneself as self-sufficient, to find one's security in oneself, instead of in God.

I stated earlier that a parallel to Paul's view of faith as trust in God's grace, was to be found even more widely in the Bible,

including the Old Testament. We have already seen how in the
Old as in the New Testament, the foundation of the life of God's
people is in God's gracious initiative. It is true that the noun
'faith' is comparatively rare in the Old Testament, and that Paul's
key text Habakkuk 2.5 may well refer to 'faithfulness' or 'enduring
loyalty' rather than purely receptive trust. But the noun 'faith' is
not completely absent in the Old Testament, and both this and the
verb 'to believe' were given peculiar significance by the prophet
Isaiah. Prophesying during the anxious time of the late eighth
century BC, with Jerusalem under increasing threat from the
Assyrians, he called the leaders of the nation to resist the tempta-
tion to rely on their own material and military strength, or the
might of neighbouring Egypt. Zion's strength and security lay in
God alone, the Holy One in the midst. 'If you will not believe,
surely you shall not be established' (Isa. 7.9). 'In returning and
rest you shall be saved; in quietness and in trust shall be your
strength' (30.15). The contrast is between self-reliance (individual
or national) and reliance upon the faithfulness of God. Moreover,
throughout the Psalms, which express the very heart of Hebrew
spirituality, there throbs the call to make the Lord one's trust.
'O Lord of hosts, blessed is the man who trusts in thee!' (Ps.
84.12).

In summary, in biblical terms the heart of faith is personal trust
which looks away from all self-sufficiency to the all-sufficiency of
the gracious God. Whatever else may be said about faith (and
much else needs to be said), if this is not grasped and made central, the reality is missed.

Where the reality of faith as sheer trust in the gracious God is
grasped, the effect is always disturbing and liberating. It is disturbing, because it is the recognition that man's security lies in
what is not himself, or of his own making, or his own possession,
and that fact puts a question-mark against all that he would make
the grounds of his self-sufficiency or pride. Not that these things
may not be good, but in themselves they are not ultimate sources
of trust. It is liberating, because it is the recognition that ultimate
reality, God, is utterly for man as Creator and Liberator. Against
all the questions posed to our worth by failure, disappointment,
suffering, and the besetting power of evil within us, there is an
unequivocal 'Yes!' to us as the persons we are. 'If God is for us,
who is against us?' asks Paul rhetorically (Rom. 8.31). There is

nothing, anywhere or at any time 'which can separate us from the love of God in Christ Jesus our Lord' (Rom. 8.39).

It is impossible to discuss the nature of faith as trust, without referring to Martin Luther. It was Luther who, at the end of the Middle Ages, and out of his own spiritual struggles and scholarly wrestling with the scriptures, rediscovered for Christianity the apostle Paul's insight and made it still more emphatic: *sola fide*, by faith alone, are we justified. More than the Reformation has flowed from this, for in recent years Luther's teaching has been appreciated at least as much by some Roman Catholic theologians as by Protestants. Protestantism has all too often allowed 'justification by faith' to become a proposition of dogmatic belief, even a new doctrinal legalism, instead of a living, inspiring reality at the heart of Christian experience. 'Faith', stated Luther, 'is a living, daring confidence in God's grace, so sure and certain that a man would stake his life upon it a thousand times. This confidence in God's grace and knowledge of it makes men glad and bold and happy in dealing with God and with all his creatures'.[2] Luther drew his biblical insights not only from Paul, but also above all from the Psalms, which, as has been said earlier in this chapter, vibrate with trust in God. Here, for instance, are three verses of Luther's paraphrase of Psalm 130.

> Our pardon is Thy gift; Thy love
>   And grace alone avail us;
> Our works could ne'er our guilt remove,
>   The strictest life would fail us;
> That none may boast himself of aught,
> But own in fear Thy grace hath wrought
>   What in him seemeth righteous.
>
> And thus my hope is in the Lord
>   And not in mine own merit;
> I rest upon His faithful word
>   To them of contrite spirit;
> That He is merciful and just –
> Here is my comfort and my trust;
>   His help I wait with patience.
>
> Though great our sins and sore our woes
>   His grace much more aboundeth;

His helping love no limit knows,
Our utmost need it soundeth;
Our kind and faithful shepherd He,
Who shall at last set Israel free
From all their sin and sorrow.

It is sometimes suggested that 'justification by faith' has little meaning for us today, because (at least as interpreted by Luther) it is an answer to the problem of individual sinfulness and guilt before God, a problem which today is nowhere near as central as it was for many people in the later Middle Ages. That in fact is disputable on the evidence supplied by clinical psychiatry. But for Luther the real issue lay not in man's sin and guilt in themselves, but in the fact that they are viewed *coram Deo*, before God, in the presence of God. It is only from God's side that they can be solved, and are solved, and therein lies the need and opportunity for that 'living, daring confidence in God's grace'. It may well be that in modern Western society the most evident spiritual need is that of finding meaning, or purpose, in life. That still means, however, that a man's need is to find a relationship to what is other than himself. 'Fulfilment' is a watchword of the hour. 'To find fulfilment', whether in intimate relationships, or work, or leisure, or wherever, is how many people would express the overriding concern of their lives. The basic issue is still whether *self*-fulfilment is really possible, or whether it is something that can only come as a gift. We can well imagine Luther, were he with us still, saying something like, 'Well, talk about "fulfilment" rather than "removal of guilt" as your chief spiritual need. But that need still has to be seen *coram Deo*. You will only find your answer in accepting God's offer of himself, in trust.'

Life in modern society displays, as much as ever, the anxious attempts of human beings to find an ultimate security in what they are in themselves, or achieve by themselves, or possess for themselves. Our ethos is that of a secularized doctrine of justification by works. Hans Küng – one of the Roman Catholic thinkers who takes justification by faith extremely seriously – writes:

In a dynamically developing world and society man attempts then to realize himself through his own achievements, not as in the former static society – although man at all times must be concerned with self-realization. Now it is only by achieving something that a person is something . . . Work, career, earning money – what could be more important? Industrializing, producing, expanding, consuming on a large or small scale, growth, progress, perfection, improvement in living standards in every respect: is not this the meaning of life? How is man to justify his existence if not by achievements? The economic values rank uppermost in the scale of values, profession and ability determine social status. By being oriented to prosperity and achievement the industrial nations can escape the pressure of primitive poverty, and establish the welfare society.[3]

Küng points out that man is threatened in his very humanity by the ever-increasing pressure to fulfil so many demands thrust upon him in a society demanding both achievement and conformity, a society impelled by the desire for growth, and controlled by rationalization. In this context Küng sees the Christian gospel and its liberating power in calling man to a 'basic trust' in God, which assures man of a meaning to his life, a meaning higher than achievement and deeper than failure.

His life then makes sense even if, for any reason, he is not accepted by his milieu or by society: if he is destroyed by opponents and deserted by friends; if he has supported the wrong side and come to grief; if his achievements slacken and are replaced by others; if he is no more use to anyone. Even the bankrupt businessman, the utterly lonely divorcé, even the overthrown and forgotten politician, the unemployed middle-aged man, the aged prostitute or the hardened criminal in the penitentiary: all these, even no longer recognized by anyone, are still recognized by him for whom there is no respect of persons and whose judgment follows the standards of his goodness.

What then is it that ultimately counts in human life? That, healthy or sick, able to work or unable to work, strong in achievement, accustomed to success or passed over by success, guilty or innocent, a person clings unswervingly and unshakably, not only at the end but throughout his whole life, to that trust which always in the New Testament goes by the name of *faith*.[4]

There is indeed no limit to the scope of the task of translating the significance of faith into the terms of secular man's search for meaning and security. It is not just that individuals are caught up in social systems which demand achievement and self-justification. It affects corporate existence as well. Even on a world scale, the divide between east and west, made potentially horrific by the nuclear arms race, is a gigantic exercise in self-righteous special pleading on both sides. The more chauvinistic newspaper editorials in this country, and equally the propaganda material of some east European states, might just as well be introduced by the prayer, 'God, we thank thee that we are not like other states . . .'.

One would hope that the bearers of the message of faith, the communities of the Christian church, would be able to exhibit to the world actual examples of that 'living, daring confidence in God's grace'. But the idea, not to mention the reality, often proves to be as strange to those of us in the churches as to anyone else. The story of the church has repeatedly shown that religion can be the greatest barrier to a trust in grace. We think God favours us because we pray, instead of the reverse. We think that being Christian endows us with a special claim on God, an insurance policy against misfortune. We think that our spiritual security lies in regular church attendance and a modicum of moral dutifulness and respectability. Or, worse, we like to parade some extra-special sign of our spiritual status. *We* are those who are 'really converted'. *We* are those who really believe the Bible. *We* are the really orthodox. Or at the other extreme, *we* are those who are really enlightened with an up-to-date theology for the age, or *we* are those who show a real grasp of the gospel by our radical social and political stance. Experience can become another source of self-assertion and self-justification. *We* are those who have had certain extraordinary experiences of the Holy Spirit, not experienced by others who therefore are not yet Christians in the full sense. There are so many ways in which the fresh air of the gospel of grace and trust, becomes the stale, stuffy atmosphere of legalism, moralism, ecclesiastical self-satisfaction and religious superiority.

Perhaps greater impact would be made by the churches, if their communities were to be seen primarily not as hives of busy activity, whether evangelistic or social, nor as earnest schools of teaching, whether traditional or avant-garde, but as springs and pools of quiet, thankful *joy*, consisting of people who have found their security and fulfilment in the God and Father of Jesus Christ, God who is utterly for man, and thus utterly to be trusted.

4

Faith as a Gift

Faith is personal trust in the graciousness of God towards us, seen in Jesus Christ. As such, it is the believer's own trust. *I* believe in God. *I* rest myself on his love as my only ultimate and lasting security. Left like that, it may sound as though faith is simply something I do, or an attitude which I take up. That I myself am fully involved in my faith, and that it represents a real decision on my part, is indeed the case, and the element of personal decision in faith is something that we shall deal with in the next chapter. But the peculiarity of faith does not allow it to be seen just as a human act or attitude.

On the other hand, the frequent orthodox assertion that faith is a supernatural affair, the gift and creation of God himself in the soul of the believer, has to be examined with some care. Taken to extremes, especially under Calvinistic influence, it can even be suggested that to 'call for a decision' in an evangelistic sense pre-empts the work of the Holy Spirit and is derogatory to the all-sufficient work of Christ who not only offered himself as an aton-ing sacrifice on our behalf but also acted as 'believer' in our stead. The motive behind such a view is sound enough. It is a fear lest faith become regarded as yet another 'work', or independent pos-session of a person, and so a means of 'boasting' or self-justification before God. That indeed is a danger – once the heart of faith as sheer trust in God's grace is forgotten. For such trust, by its very nature, is at once the recognition that God is all-sufficient for salvation, and, obversely, that the believer in himself is no-thing. The last thing that faith can do, therefore, is to regard *itself* as worthy of any merit. Faith means looking away entirely from oneself to God. But it is a looking, and, to that extent, a human act.

If it can be borne in mind that the essence of faith as trust lies in its being an actual relationship of the believer to God, there is no real difficulty in seeing how faith is both the trust of a person and yet the gift of God. If, however, faith is seen primarily as an intellectual understanding *about* God, or some emotional state or feeling which arises when religious affairs are brought to mind, then the claim that faith is a gift of divine grace certainly looks suspicious. For it then appears as if, on the one hand, normal human functions of mind and will are suspended, and that grace comes in as an impersonal force subverting human freedom and bending the mind in a certain direction, almost as if a super-natural drug was being injected, or a pair of electrodes, plugged into heaven, was being implanted in the brain. This makes it look either as though God rides rough-shod over normal and healthy human consciousness, or that faith tries to substantiate itself as a quite arbitrary and irrational opinion by appealing to divine inter-vention as the basis of its assurance. It is worth recalling the ironical comments of that sceptical thinker, David Hume.

> So that, upon the whole, we may conclude, that the *Christian religion* not only was at first attended with miracles, but even at this day cannot be believed by any reasonable person without one. Mere reason is insufficient to convince us of its veracity. And whoever is moved by *Faith* to assent to it, is conscious of a continued miracle in his own person, which subverts all the principles of his understanding, and gives him a determination to believe what is most contrary to custom and experience.[1]

But faith does not involve some kind of divine brain-washing. Nor is it on the other hand purely an act of human self-will, an assertion or choice to believe in some arbitrary way. It arises in relationship, and therewith its nature as both a gift and a free act of trust is to be understood.

In chapter 2 I suggested that there is a close parallel between faith as trust in God, and many instances over the whole range of human experience where we are related to realities other than our-selves in a trustful, appreciative way. It was also argued that even in those so-called ordinary instances our attitude of trust or appreciation is not simply generated from within ourselves, but in

a real sense is evoked in us by those realities. Our sense of wonder
at the view from the mountain top, or the delight in a Mozart sym-
phony, or the excitement at the match-winning goal, are ours; but
we could not have produced them on our own. They require the
things *to which they are responses*. Being responses, they owe themselves to these objects at least as much as to ourselves. Most of all
this applies in our relationships with other persons. In having a
friend, it is not simply that I maintain an attitude of trust and
appreciation towards him. It is he who evokes it in me. Dr Johnson advised that a man should keep his friendships in repair. But
there is a limit to which a friendship can be 'cultivated'. It
requires a great deal of receptivity on our part, a sheer openness
to what is being offered to us.

Faith as trust in God has a gift-character because of its profoundly relational nature. Basically, we can trust in God because
he actually makes himself available to us as trustworthy, and
invites our trust. It is because he moves towards us, that we owe it
all to him. The God whom faith apprehends is not just an idea to
be thought about or assented to. He is an actual presence encoun-
tering us in Jesus Christ, who lived and died in human history,
who appears before us whenever his story is told again, and who is
proclaimed by the church as Lord of all. Faith therefore finds
itself evoked by a very specific and concrete reality, both transcendent and historical. It finds in Jesus Christ a truth which
'compels', but compulsive in a peculiar way. God does not
directly compel us to believe in him. He respects our freedom in a
uniquely gracious way. But such is this graciousness, such is his
own nature as gracious love, that he reveals himself to us for what
he is. It is precisely this graciousness which we find 'compelling' –
compelling in itself, not because any constraints other than this
graciousness are applied to us. A truth becomes compelling when
it makes its own appeal to us and we accept it on its own terms,
without being badgered into assenting to it under other authorities or threats. There is a real acceptance on our part, but we do
not hail our acceptance as our cleverness at having seen the truth.
Rather, we acclaim the truth as being clearly true. A British theologian of a former generation, John Oman, who had such profound insight into the way in which as persons we are dealt with
by the gracious God, wrote:

The right beginning is not faith as an emotion concerned about itself, but faith as a trust relying upon God. Only as faith arises from an object which constrains belief is it truly faith, being, by so much as it is of our own effort, the less faith. Only when, on contemplation of the object, belief constrains us, and we have no need to constrain it, is faith real. Except in so far as it impresses us as true, we have no right to believe anything; and to try to impress ourselves in a direction contrary to the object itself is to forget that truth is the basis of all right moral motive, and reality the security of all religious history. A true faith is simply faith in the truth solely because it convinces us that it is true.[2]

So faith as personal trust in the graciousness of God has no option but to regard itself as being evoked by and therefore a gift of that graciousness which has evoked it, and towards which it is directed. There are no magical tricks here, but certainly wonder and gratitude which cry: To God be the glory.

Direct references to faith as the gift or creation of God are not to be found in the New Testament quite as frequently as the works of some later theologians might suggest. Such references as there are mostly seem surprisingly casual. Peter, addressing the apostles and elders in Jerusalem on the subject of the conversion of the gentiles says that God 'made no distinction between us and them, but cleansed their hearts by faith' (Acts 15.9). Paul mentions some who are endowed, in an apparently particular way, with 'faith' as one of the diverse manifestations of the Spirit among the members of the Christian community (I Cor. 12.9). The Letter to the Ephesians concludes with the blessing: 'Peace be to the brethren and love with faith, from God the Father and the Lord Jesus Christ' (Ephes. 6.23). What seems to have chiefly concerned the New Testament writers was less the relationship between the divine and human elements in faith, than what actually occasions faith. Significant here are Paul's words: 'So faith comes from what is heard, and what is heard comes by the preaching of Christ' (Rom. 10.17). The New English Bible expresses it slightly more vividly: 'We conclude that faith is awakened by the message, and the message that awakens it comes through the word of Christ.' 'So we preached, and so you believed', Paul writes elsewhere (I Cor. 15.11). Rudolf Bultmann summarizes the specifically

Christian understanding of faith on this basis, as 'the acceptance of the kerygma of Christ'.[3]

With certain important qualifications, especially regarding the Fourth Gospel and the letters of John, it can be said that in the New Testament the noun 'faith' or the verb 'to believe' are mostly used with Greek prepositions rendered in English by 'in'. One believes *in* God, *in* Christ, *in* the message of God's act in Christ, and this indicates the deeply existential relation between the believer and God in his self-disclosure. There is an unspoken but very evident difference between this type of faith and a basically intellectualistic credence, a 'belief that'. At the immediate, concrete level one is not presented with an idea to be idly contemplated or speculated upon, but a message, the 'good news' (*euangelion*) or 'proclamation' (*kerygma*), which addresses itself to the deepest questions of everyone's existence. We have summarized the content of this message in the previous chapter, in describing Jesus as the climactic offer of God's graciousness to us. The message of God's grace in Christ is what one believes in, and the message itself is what evokes faith. All along, therefore, faith has a gift-character, being a response of trusting acceptance of the God who has acted in Jesus Christ, and who now presents us with those actions through the message concerning them.

We do not, therefore, invent faith for ourselves, or conjure it up by an effort of will within us. In Jesus, conveyed to us in the message about him, we are presented with God's graciousness, and we are invited to accept. To accept it is to enter into a personal relationship of trust in the God who so presents himself. It is, in effect, to say to God: 'You, God, whose graciousness I see in Jesus, and whom Jesus showed by his life, death and resurrection to be worthy of all trust, are my sole trust, security and guide, in life and in death. Faced with you as you are, I cannot but trust you.'

Ronald Gregor Smith summarized all this superbly: 'an existential faith is a unity in relation of the Giver of faith and the believer'.[4] Not that the 'unity in relation' between God and the believer can be understood as some kind of mystical fusion or even, as a theologian like Emil Brunner was wont to stress, purely as an 'encounter' in an 'I-Thou' type of relation. For again, as Gregor Smith repeatedly emphasized, the historical person of Jesus and the message about him cannot be allowed to drop out of the picture. For Christian faith, the relationship with Jesus is not just a stage on the way to the relationship with 'God himself', which can be discarded and left behind once the soul is face to face with 'God himself'. Jesus is himself the climax of God's graciousness in history, and whoever would grasp the God of grace must grasp Jesus, the Word made flesh.

Further, as was pointed out in the previous chapter, Jesus is not only the proclaimer, and not only the embodiment, of God's grace. He is also the one who embodies the fullest human response to that grace, in one and the same movement. 'And being found in human form, he humbled himself, and became obedient unto death, even death on a cross' (Phil. 2.8). He is, in Paul's language, the 'second Adam' whose perfect trust, loyalty and obedience to God marks a new beginning for human existence hitherto characterized by the disloyalty, self-sufficiency and self-seeking symbolized in the story of the trespass of the 'first Adam'. In Gerhard Ebeling's apt summary phrases, Jesus is the 'basis' and 'witness' of faith.[5] Jesus, in other words, is himself the true believer, and the absolute trust in God which is invited and required of us in face of the cross of Jesus, means what can only be described as a *participation* in Jesus himself. Jesus is the *enabler* of our faith in God, through our personal attachment to him in discipleship. More than an abrupt 'encounter' of an I-Thou kind is indicated here. Truly personal relationships involve more than 'encounters'. They involve some kind of 'side-by-side' relationships as well as 'face-to-face' meetings. Acquaintances become friends, lovers become life-partners, as they share experiences and undertake commitments to each other and *with* each other. They come to share a common destiny in part of their lives at least. They take part in making piece of human history together. The relationship grows because their attention is not simply focussed on each other, but *together* it is focussed on something other than themselves, whether in play, or in the making of a home, or something more grandiose like political activity.

The believer enters into a 'side-by-side', as well as a 'face-to-face' relationship with Jesus Christ. He finds himself invited to share with Jesus in the destiny of one who depends solely on the grace of God, as child to parent. Paul expresses this most profoundly in terms of the working of the Spirit:

For all who are led by the Spirit of God are sons of God. For you did not receive the spirit of slavery to fall back into fear, but you have received the spirit of sonship. When we cry 'Abba! Father!' it is the Spirit himself bearing witness with our spirit that we are children of God, and if children, then heirs, heirs of God and fellow-heirs with Christ, provided we suffer with him that we may also be glorified with him.

(Rom. 8.14–17. Cf: Gal. 4.6f.).

'Abba!' seems to have been the peculiarly intimate name by which Jesus himself addressed God in prayer. The English equivalent of this Aramaic word might almost be 'Daddy!': the word by which an infant addresses his or her father in confident trust. To have such a trust in God is enabled through attachment to Jesus, who by his life of humble, obedient service even to the cross lived out this trust to its uttermost limits, and whose trust was finally vindicated in the resurrection. Faith therefore means trusting in Jesus and sharing his trust in the Father. Faith is a life of participation in the destiny of Jesus, shaped by the 'Abba!' kind of trust. And this participation in Jesus comes as a gift to us, something we are *enabled* to enter into, and this is what is indicated by 'Spirit'. To repeat what has been said earlier, trust, appreciation, wonder, are responses evoked in us by realities other than ourselves. We do not just see such evocative realities in a detached way. We become caught up with them and open to them in a kind of *communion*. It is not just a case of there being two separate entities, oneself and the thing to which one responds. The experience of communion and participation indicates that there is some kind of connecting, communicative medium between ourselves and that which evokes our response. This 'between' is what, following Martin Buber, Ronald Gregor Smith and John Taylor, is the realm of active spirit and, we may dare to say, Holy Spirit. Holy Spirit is the power by which we are made aware of persons and things other than ourselves, and supremely makes us aware of God himself as revealed through Jesus Christ. Holy Spirit's activity is seen in Jesus himself, in his life and death of utter graciousness, and his absolute trust in God. Holy Spirit is the bond of unity between Jesus and the Father in whom he trusted. It is the inner reality of which the cry 'Abba! Father!' is the outer expression. But further, Holy Spirit is the attractive power which evokes our response to Jesus, and with Jesus to the Father in that 'side-by-side' relationship with the utterly trusting and obedient Christ. Our relationship to God the Father is thus one into which we are graciously invited and enabled to enter, for it is the relationship already created by Jesus in his life and death. Faith as trust in God is thus a deeply personal relationship to God through and with Jesus Christ, evoked in us and offered to us as a gift of participation, and in this sense from start to finish faith is a gift. Here is the profundity which lies behind Paul's statement that no one can confess 'Jesus is Lord' unless speaking 'by the Holy Spirit' (I Cor. 12.9).

To summarize what has been said in this chapter, faith as trust in God is a gift of God since it is a personal relationship to him, a relationship of trustful sonship enabled by our participation in and with Jesus' relation of sonship to his Father. To understand faith as an independent possession of the believer – whether an intellectual understanding, or an emotion, or an effort of will – outside this actual relationship is a gross error which leads to all kinds of confusions. For instance, if faith is assumed to be primarily an intellectual assertion about the existence of a Creator who is responsible for the world as we know it, entanglement in certain philosophical questions results at the wrong level. The sceptical philosopher may query the meaning of a statement such as 'The world is the creation of a wise and loving God', and ask just how such a view may be verified or disproved. Just how much weight of contrary 'evidence' will such a statement stand? How hideous must the picture of suffering, evil and sheer moral indifference in the universe, be drawn before such a belief becomes untenable? The apparent refusal of some believers to answer this challenge directly, appears to the sceptical philosopher as at best naive, at worst perverse. Faith appears to be wilful self-delusion which is not even prepared to come out into the open and be tested against facts. Faith certainly should face facts, but this kind of criticism fails to perceive what is the central reality to which faith attaches. Faith does not primarily rest itself on a concept of God and the universe as his creation, as a tenable hypothesis. It does not live by such a detached, spectatorial attitude. Faith apprehends itself to be an actual, living relationship with the God who is not a shadowy possibility at the far end of an argument, but the utterly real and personal Presence bursting through into communication with us in our history. For the believer, it is not simply that God exists, but that God has moved towards him in Jesus and created with him a new relationship which on the God-ward side is one of grace, and on the human side one of trusting grasp of that grace. The relationship itself is a gift of grace, and for the believer it is the great reality at the centre of his experience from which all else is viewed. It is not, therefore, that the believer is naive or perverse when, despite so much seeming evidence to the contrary, he still holds to belief in a gracious God. For nothing can take away from him his sense of having entered, with Jesus Christ, into a filial relationship with God, a relationship which *includes* suffering as part of its destiny. 'Abba, Father, all things are possible to thee; remove this cup from me; yet not what I will, but what thou wilt' (Mark 14.36). '. . . fellow heirs with Christ, provided we suffer with him that we may also be glorified with him' (Rom. 8.17). And were the world bathed in universal pleasure, with pain and evil redundant words, so that the idea of a beneficent Creator appeared more rationally 'tenable', it would still be the case that *faith* lives in its own integrity, as a personal relationship of trust in the gracious God. In good or ill, faith is not primarily a matter of ideas. It is a personal response to that utterly gracious reality which faces us in Jesus Christ.

5

Faith as Decision

Faith, we have seen, is neither a purely human act or attitude, nor some wholly unnatural creation of God. It is a personal relationship between a trusting human person and the gracious God, a relationship which is itself due to that graciousness. Yet the human element cannot be ignored. In essence, it is trust. But this must further be characterized as founded upon the *decision* to trust. At first, it might seem as though we are now moving into the area of human psychology rather than theology, and that therefore this aspect of faith would be more amenable to straightforward description than the theme of the previous chapter. In fact, the nature of faith as decision is not nearly so straightforward as might be supposed. For here we are talking about one of the most intimate aspects of our own being as human persons, that of making choices, and 'objectivity' is necessarily limited. We cannot wholly get outside ourselves to look at ourselves. Without wishing to be unduly obscurantist, we have to recognize that we are here dealing with something which ultimately eludes exact analysis and explanation.

The late Ronald Gregor Smith, whose words we quoted in the previous chapter as aptly summarizing the nature of faith as a 'unity in relation' between God and the believer, was one who, despite all his profound insight and lifelong wrestling with the question, saw how difficult it is to give a satisfying account as to how and *why* one takes the decision of faith. Once, in a radio discussion with an agnostic, J. P. Corbett, he said:

I should say it is a decision one takes – perhaps that is not the right expression either – or even a choice that one makes, a risk that one has to undergo, in a situation that is really quite unparalleled . . . I see the veiled coming of God in Christ, not as a mere bolt from the blue or anything like that, but as corresponding to the actual kind of human situation that you yourself described in the situation in relation to the neighbour. I can only say that I am afraid there seems to be some kind of threshold here, an invisible door through this transparent wall that seems to be dividing us, through which I go. There is here a decision that simply is of some strange and unique kind.[1]

Corbett's response was equally interesting:

The fact of the matter is, that you have got something inside yourself, what you call your faith, and also what you express in certain words in company with fellow-believers, which you think is of supreme importance . . . It does not seem to get between us, and yet that you have this faith is of supreme importance to you, and that I have not got it seems obviously to you to mark a profound lack in me.[2]

This is a conversation between two people who see themselves and their world in a fundamentally different way, however close their attitudes and ethical stances may be over a wide range of human issues. For Corbett the agnostic, the meaning of life centres around the importance of relationships with other persons. For Gregor Smith the Christian, such relationships are important as the medium through which something else is encountered, namely, the gracious self-giving of God to us, as disclosed in Jesus Christ. For the Christian, to view reality in this way results from a decision, but not an arbitrary or self-willed one. It is a free response to what he sees has been given to him, to what has faced him in Jesus Christ. So Gregor Smith could in one instance define faith as 'the free response to the forgiving word of God which frees us to live in the world for God's future'.[3] It is a choice made in freedom – not an abstract freedom *in vacuo,* but a freedom which is in face of the message which calls for a decision. As to *why* one decides for faith very little can be said, except that one finds God's graciousness in Jesus Christ to be the compelling truth, and that one gives oneself to accept it as the truth.

If, when pressed to the limit, there still remains an element of irreducible mystery in such a decision, this has to be accepted as one of the facts of our life as persons. To be human involves making choices on issues ranging from the trivial and commonplace to those which can determine the whole direction of our lives. We can give 'rational' grounds by which we can justify our decisions as sound or sensible, and if life is not to dissolve into meaningless chaos we have to. But the 'reasons' we give for our decisions do not ultimately account for the fact that we actually take those decisions. Suppose, for example, that I have to travel by car from Bristol to Gloucester. I have the option of using either the M5 motorway or the old main road, the A38. If my time is limited, I will most likely use the M5 on the grounds that it is the quickest route. If, however, I have more time, if it is a nice day and the Gloucestershire villages will be looking at their springtime best, I may well take the A38. To the question 'Why?' in relation to either of these routes, I can give rational grounds as answers. The answers are in terms of one's responsibilities to diary engagements, petrol consumption and personal enjoyment. But the fact remains that I could, in practice, decide to use the A38 when the M5 on rational grounds would be the sensible route, and that I could in fact burn up the M5 when I could perfectly well enjoy the A38. So even if I do the 'rational' thing, the *reason* I do it is because I *choose* to be rational. Of course, the freedom which a person has to exercise choice can be over-emphasized as in some extreme forms of existentialism, where truth virtually becomes 'what I decide to think is true' or simply 'true for me'. Truth is not made for us by ourselves. But it is recognized, and the acceptance of what we recognize as true is a decision. This is a fine, but crucial, distinction. The acceptance of truth is a free decision, but not therefore an arbitrary one. And the fact that we may find the truth 'compelling' does not contradict our acceptance of it as a free, personal decision.

The act of deciding, in itself, is hidden from us. It is rather like that odd physiological phenomenon of looking at one's face in a mirror and directing one's gaze at one's left eye, then switching the gaze to the right eye. The actual movement of the eyes is never seen by oneself. One moment, one is looking in one direction, the next moment in another. So too in the business of 'making up one's mind' we can never say 'At this moment, I am deciding for this as against that'. We say 'I haven't yet decided', or 'I have decided'. The moment of decision is a point to which we move, or move on from, but never actually comprehend. It is as if at that point all our personal energies are concentrated into the most intense exercise of our personal being (that is, making a free choice), that there is no part of the self which can be spared for the superfluous activity of watching it. At that point, one simply *is*. We remember the 'before' and are conscious of the 'now', and know that there has been a divide which is our own responsibility. That is all.

Or we might say that making a decision is like a moment of death, death out of which comes a new birth. For in making a decision we end the state of mind in which we have been hitherto, with its possible choices before us, and we embark on a new stage of life, set on the one possibility that has been chosen. In the moment of death, we are hidden from ourselves, and emerge to a new consciousness of what are to be and do. To move through life via such stages of death-and-birth is one of the marks of personal existence, for a person is not made once and for all, but lives in a process of continual emergence, of continuity through change. John Macquarrie writes:

> To use a familiar figure, we can think of the individual standing before a block of uncarved stone. That block is the sum total of his potentialities, and out of it he has to sculpt a meaningful life. He does that by his decisions, and every 'de-cision' is a cutting away; that is to say, it is a decision against as well as a decision for, it means relinquishing one possibility to take up another. The one relinquished may be something for which the person is very well fitted, as when he weighs two possible careers, knowing that he might have much to contribute in either of them, yet knowing also that he must choose one to the exclusion of the other. Every decision is, in a sense, a death – it is discarding something that might have been part of one's life. But this is precisely how a life, on the plane of finite existence, must be lived . . .[4]

No one emphasized so sharply the element of decision in truly human life, and in Christian life above all, as did Søren Kierkegaard. He was oppressed by the sense that his contemporary society in nineteenth-century Denmark had forgotten that to be a man meant being a 'single person', an individual who accepts responsibility for himself before God. One has to *decide*, with all possible passion, what one is to be and to do. On the social level, Kierkegaard felt, people were submerging their unique individuality in the attitudes of the crowd. Intellectually, they were losing sight of the wonder and uniqueness of the human person and his choices, so captivated were they by the concept of the universe as a single, unfolding rational system as portrayed in Hegel's philosophy. Spiritually, they were equating Christianity with commonplace notions about God's goodness and human benevolence, forgetting the awesome truth that between God and man there is an 'infinite qualitative difference', and ignoring the abysmal depths of human sin and guilt in face of divine holiness. Kierkegaard's whole life and work is a challenge to come out of the unthinking assumptions and conventions of life in the mass, and to take one's own existence in hand, however painful this might be.

Perhaps Kierkegaard saw so clearly the importance of personal decision in human existence that he underplayed the equally important aspect of existence as relationship with other persons. He saw an either/or divide between the sub-human 'mass' or crowd, and the authentically existing 'single one', without fully recognizing that there can and should be a *communal* existence in which people afford each other their full status and dignity as persons – an existence which Martin Buber characterized as a 'binding' together as distinct from a mere 'bundling' together in the mass. Nevertheless, it is to Kierkegaard's credit that he did discern so profoundly the decisive nature of human existence, and his insight has proved to be the source of so much 'existential' thinking in the twentieth century. It is an insight which is necessary to counterbalance the view, derived from a slick reading of Marx, that human beings are entirely the product of their environment. Important for our immediate purpose here, in his most substantial work *The Concluding Unscientific Postscript* there is a remark in which Kierkegaard simply yet brilliantly captures what happens when a person makes a decision. He speaks of 'the individual, by an internal decision, putting an end to mere possibility, and identifying himself with the content of his thought in order to exist in it'.[5] A decision is thus more than an act of the intellect, although the intellect is certainly involved. It is a turning, a movement, of one's very self. What was formerly a possible action or attitude, or one of several possibilities which might be adopted, is now embraced as the reality by which one's actual existence is to be determined. We often say, quite significantly, when trying to come to a decision 'I see several possibilities *before* me'. It is as though one is a spectator of the various options being paraded in front of oneself on some kind of mental television screen. Mentally, we adopt a kind of role-play to try to visualize what would be experienced if we adopted these possibilities, in turn. Having decided, the situation changes completely. It is not that there is now one 'possibility' before us on the screen. There are no *possibilities* at all, and the screen has disappeared. We have passed through it. We are no longer observers. We are already on the way into the next stage of life, in the direction set by the course of action we have chosen. It is no longer role-play, but the real thing, for better or worse. We have, as Kierkegaard put it, identified ourselves with the content of our thought, in order to exist in it. It is no longer before us, but part of us.

Faith, as personal trust in God through Jesus Christ, is reached through decision. It is a decision for the utter reliability of God's grace as our only final security, a decision to respond personally to his movement to us as seen in Jesus. This has of course been particularly stressed in the 'evangelical' traditions within Christianity, which always serve to remind that faith cannot be identified with mere intellectual credence about the existence of God, or a preference for 'good' behaviour as against 'bad'. There is a discontinuity between faith and all that precedes it. Faith, as Kierkegaard put it, means a leap. No intellectual argument of itself can lead directly to faith. Intellectual argument for the existence of God, for the truth and relevance of the Christian message, for the effect which faith has had on the lives of its adherents (or some of them), can all point in a certain direction. They may point to faith as a quite rational possibility. They may even bring a person to the point of seeing the Christian message as a beckoning and even compelling truth. But there comes a point where the person must decide, must venture, risk and entrust himself in answer to the invitation that is given to him. It means, using Kierkegaard's words again, putting an end to God and his grace as a possibility, and actually identifying with it and existing in it.

The nature of faith as decision stems not only from its being an instance of the decisive nature of human existence in general. Much more profoundly, the decisiveness of faith is required by the reality in which faith trusts, that is, in God. The invitation to faith is the invitation to rest for one's worth and security entirely in the One who is utterly other than us, yet utterly for us. God is not another thing or person in the world, nor to be treated as such. He is other, transcendent, and yet in his otherness and transcendence he is present to us. He is holy, and he is in our midst. Were he holy and far off, faith could be a matter of calm, donnish speculation over the port. Were he near yet not so holy, not so different, less majestic, faith could be a pleasant affair of bright and trivial chatter and good intentions. But God being holy *and* present, faith is a desperately serious affair. It is the great crisis. With God, we are up against what is ultimately and eternally real, and how we are to relate to that ultimate and eternal reality is the question of our own eternal destiny. He offers himself in his grace to be received in trust. To accept is to accept a life with God, which nothing can take away, in life or in death. To refuse is to choose to maintain ourselves in our self-contained existence, which has no ultimate future. The use of the word 'crisis' a few sentences ago was not accidental, for the Greek *krisis* means judgment. Faced with God, we know we are under judgment. We are questioned about our aims of justifying and fulfilling ourselves by our own resources and for our own ends. Faced with the Holy One, the One who is alone ultimately real, we have to decide for his grace as our life, which is salvation, or ourselves, which is death. Whatever we make of the traditional doctrines and imagery of heaven and hell, a creeping trivialization of the meaning of human life sets in if we lose our hold upon the vision of a God who is working with an ultimate purpose for the lives of men and nations. That God is gracious means that he does will to give himself to us as our God for ever. But grace is no easy-going benevolence. It is an undeserved, unmerited self-giving of the Holy One, the Creator to his creatures. It cannot be presumed upon, and to disregard it is an awesome responsibility. Equally, to accept it is a drastic leap. It means a de-cision, a cutting away, of all the alternative possibilities in which we are tempted to find ultimate meaning, satisfaction and security. It means looking away from ourselves and what we are, or have, or might do, as our real hope. The decision of faith thus goes beyond

all others we can make. To decide what to do is often hard enough
in ordinary life. To decide that the ground of our life is not in
what we can do for ourselves, but in what God does with us and
for us, seems like the decision to saw off the one plank we have
left to stand on. Hence Kierkegaard's vivid description of faith
as a man struggling on 70,000 fathoms of ocean. Yet, if he does
not struggle, but rests, the ocean will support him.

The decisiveness of faith is etched throughout the Bible. In the
Old Testament the 'chosen people' are not allowed unthinkingly
to assume that their relationship to God is guaranteed simply by
the continued existence of the nation, or the Temple in Jerusalem,
or the succession of the descendants of King David on the throne.
God is faithful, his purpose steadfast. But that is precisely why
the people's response of loyalty, right worship and right dealings
with one another must continually be reaffirmed and renewed. To
take God's goodwill for granted, to presume upon his patience
while the people perversely followed their own wishes and fed
their complacency with insincere worship, would result in disaster
for the nation. God's faithfulness would then be manifested in
breaking up their settled existence so that they might recover
their sense of dependence and genuine trust in him. So the
prophets warned, who saw each national misfortune or calamity
as the hand of God calling his people to a new decision of trust
and loyalty. Genuine trust in God must be distinguished from
illusory reliance upon fantasies of their own making, as Micah's
trenchant words on Jerusalem made clear:

> Its heads give judgment for a bribe,
>   its priests teach for hire,
>   its prophets divine for money;
> yet they lean upon the Lord and say,
>   'Is not the Lord in the midst of us?
>   No evil shall come upon us.'
> Therefore because of you Zion shall be plowed as a field;
> Jerusalem shall become a heap of ruins,
>   and the mountain of the house a wooded height (Micah 3.11f.).

Perhaps the most dramatic instance of what the decision of faith
could mean was provided by Jeremiah, as Jerusalem was brought
under increasing pressure from the beseiging armies of Babylon:

And to this people you shall say: 'Thus says the Lord: Behold,

I have set before you the way of life and the way of death. He who stays in this city shall die by the sword, by famine and by pestilence; but he who goes out and surrenders to the Chaldeans who are besieging you shall live and shall have his life as a prize of war' (Jer. 21.8–9).

To an overconfident, chauvinistic military regime, such talk sounded defeatist, subversive and sheer madness. Yet as events showed, Jeremiah had truly discerned that the way to life was to be found through the way of apparent surrender and death. Faith is of that order of decisiveness.

Nowhere is this decisiveness found more clearly than in Jesus and his teaching. In an earlier chapter I argued against the popular view that the idea of a God of love is foreign to the Old Testament. Equally, the note of awesome decision is not absent from the New. Whoever looks to the gospels solely for comfort must face the flaming challenge of Jesus:

Do not think that I have come to bring peace on earth; I have not come to bring peace, but a sword. For I have come to set a man against his father, and a daughter against her mother, and a daughter-in-law against her mother-in-law; and a man's foes will be those of his own household. He who loves father or mother more than me is not worthy of me; and he who loves son or daughter more than me is not worthy of me; and he who does not take his cross and follow me is not worthy of me. He who finds his life will lose it, and he who loses his life for my sake will find it (Matt. 10.34–39).

Jesus' ministry focussed on calling people to decide for God in face of his coming kingdom. 'Repent, and believe in the gospel' (Mark 1.15). Repentance (*metanoia*) means turning around, a complete re-orientation of one's existence. The depth of its meaning is seen when it is set alongside the sayings about losing one's life in order to find it. Repentance means much more, therefore, than a desire for moral self-betterment. It means a total abnegation of one's own desires and claims, in face of the unparalleled mercy of God which is coming to reign, an utter submission in trust and gratitude.

Repentance of sin, which traditionally has been seen as such a central feature of the decision for faith, has to be seen in the light of what sin itself really is. Sin both is, and is much more than, the sum total of one's moral misdemeanours and failures. Its full theological meaning is that of a turning away from God himself, an attempt to live one's life apart from him, in self-sufficiency. It is the attempt to set oneself up in an independent existence, for oneself. To repent means to turn from this self-orientated existence (which may in fact try to disguise itself in a very religious and devout life), to trust in the gracious God, who alone is truly good (Mark 10.18). Repentance and trust are therefore two aspects of the same movement of decision.

It is no accident that we have been able to describe any real decision as a kind of death leading to new life, and that in the New Testament the decision of faith is so often described as the supreme experience of dying and living again, of losing one's life and finding it anew. To relinquish all claims for oneself, to look beyond all finite and worldly securities, is truly to die. And to find in the trusting relationship to God, through Christ, an absolute assurance of worth and meaning is to live again on a new and re-orientated plane. So Paul can write:

> I have been crucified with Christ; it is no longer I who live, but Christ who lives in me; and the life I now live in the flesh I live by faith in the Son of God, who loved me and gave himself for me (Gal. 2.20).

To decide for trust in the gracious God is thus a momentous decision, the most momentous that a person can ever make. It is the decision to let go of ourselves entirely, to forego all security in ourselves and in what we can make of ourselves in the world, in accepting the grace of him who alone can secure us in life and in death. To trust in God cannot therefore be a bland, nodding acceptance of his favour. That, in Bonhoeffer's words, turns grace into 'cheap grace'. Grace is costly, for if our hand would grasp the mercy of God, our hand must cease clutching as its fondest possession our own heart, that inmost centre of ourselves which would love to live independently and take the credit for its self-sufficiency. To let go of itself, stooping under its pride and leaping beyond its anxieties, is the hardest move which the human heart can make. In fact it cannot make it, but for the initiative of the movement of grace towards it, beckoning and enabling in relationship. It is in this situation that the decision is taken, deeply costly from the human side, yet also ascribed to the working of God's grace. As Luther put it:

What does a man reach who hopes in God, save his own nothingness? But whither shall a man vanish, who vanishes into nothingness, except to where he came from? He came from God and from his own nothingness. So he who returns to nothingness returns to God. For he who falls outside himself and all creatures, whom God's hand embraces, cannot fall out of God's hand. For he holds the whole world in his hands, says Isaiah. Fall then through the whole world – whither do you fall? Into the hand and the lap of God.[6]

None of this implies that the process of 'conversion' always means a climactic wrestling of the soul before God, a traumatic experience of emotional stress and a grand, once-for-all decision. For some, that is the case. For others, it may appear to be a much less dramatic affair. For many people the story of faith is one of a succession of 'conversions' in which at successively deeper levels the discovery is made of the need and the offer of grace. Each confrontation with a new challenge, each new realization of one's stubbornness, pride, misguided ambitions or flight from responsibility, can be the occasion of a new decision for trust in the God who claims us. Nevertheless, for many Christians there is one particular moment in their lives to which they can look back, a mysterious moment marking the divide between faith as a possibility, and faith as an actuality, the moment of decision. It may or may not have been particularly 'emotional'. Certainly, no one set of emotions can be regarded as criteria for the genuineness of the decision. There is, on the one hand, the testimony of those who record an immediate sense of spiritual uplift and joy, such as John Wesley described on that night when his heart became 'strangely warmed' in Aldersgate. On the other hand, here is C. S. Lewis's laconic account of the final stage of his journey to full acceptance of Christian faith.

At each step one had less chance 'to call one's soul one's own'. To accept the Incarnation was a further step in the same direction. It brings God nearer, or near in a new way. And this, I found, was something I had not wanted. But to recognise the ground for my evasion was of course to recognise both its shame and its futility. I know very well when, but hardly how, the final step was taken. I was driven to Whipsnade one sunny morning. When we set out I did not believe that Jesus Christ is the Son of God, and when we reached the zoo I did. Yet I had not exactly spent the journey in thought. Nor in great emotion. 'Emotional' is perhaps the last word we can apply to some of the most important events. It was more like when a man, after long sleep, lying motionless in bed, becomes aware that he is now awake. And it was like that moment on top of the bus, ambiguous. Freedom, or necessity? Or do they differ at their maximum? At that maximum a man is what he does; there is nothing of him left over or outside the act. As for what we commonly call Will, and what we commonly call Emotion, I fancy these usually talk too loud, protest too much, to be quite believed, and we have a secret suspicion that the great passion or the iron resolution is partly a put-up job.[7]

Less important than 'emotion' is the decision itself, hidden from us in its mysterious mechanism, but re-orientating our being from self-reliance to God-reliance. Aversion to certain types of evangelism which play too heavily upon the emotions should not therefore be an excuse for playing down the nature of Christian proclamation as calling for decision. That decision cannot be pressured or manipulated, but in all its momentousness it has in some way and at some point to be invited. Christianity cannot simply be equated with a broadening of moral outlook, or an injection of idealism, or an intensifying of religious emotion. Its central symbols are a cross and an empty tomb. It revolves around an end and a new beginning, and this infects even the apprehension of the message. For it is the decision, in face of the utter grace of God, to allow God to be all and oneself to be nothing, in order that one may be somebody in a new way.

6

Faith as Confession

So far it has been stressed that faith is deeply personal, a relationship of trust in the God who embraces us with his grace as seen in Jesus. It is entered upon by an 'internal decision', whereby the very core of our being is moved away from self-reliance to rest in God as our security. From this, it might appear that faith is a purely 'inward' affair, something wholly 'spiritual', relating only to our 'inmost soul'. That it does so reach down into the depths of our being is true. But to say that it is personal means that it involves the whole scope of our existence as persons. There is an outer as well as an inner aspect to each of us, and truly personal existence requires an integration between the two.

Any view of faith which sees only the 'inward' aspect is brought up short by Paul's statement: 'If you confess with your lips that Jesus is Lord and believe in your heart that God raised him from the dead, you will be saved. For man believes with his heart and so is justified, and he confesses with his lips and so is saved' (Rom. 10.9f.). The first sentence jars on the prevailing modern religious ethos, for it seems to give priority to a merely verbal utterance at the expense of the 'real' business of believing with the heart. And even the second sentence, which admittedly puts belief of the heart before utterance with the lips, still attaches equal (saving!) significance to the verbal confession. Paul would probably not have understood our modern qualms at all. With his Jewish outlook, emphasizing as it did humanity as a unity of spirit, mind and body, he would not have seen the reality of faith simply as a matter of either heart *or* lips, will *or* statement. Man is a whole, and his faith reflects the unity between inner and outer.

Behind Paul's statement here lies the Old Testament saying: 'But the word is very near you; it is in your mouth and in your heart, so that you can do it' (Deut. 30.14). The Old Testament, especially in the prophetic writings, certainly recognizes the danger that men can verbally profess loyalty to God without truly meaning it or understanding it, as when Jeremiah caricatured those who came to worship saying 'The temple of the Lord, the temple of the Lord'. But equally, it was the Hebraic assumption that those who trusted in God would verbally and in other outward ways express that faith. Notice how concrete this expression is seen to be in the following passage.

When you come into the land which the Lord your God gives you for an inheritance and have taken possession of it, and live in it, you shall take some of the first of all the fruit of the ground, which you harvest from your land that the Lord your God gives you, and you shall put it in a basket, and you shall go to the place which the Lord your God will choose, to make his name to dwell there. And you shall go to the priest who is in office at that time, and say to him, 'I declare this day to the Lord your God that I have come into the land which the Lord swore to your fathers to give us.' Then the priest shall take the basket from your hand, and set it down before the altar of the Lord your God. And you shall make response before the Lord your God, 'A wandering Aramean was my father; and he went down into Egypt and sojourned there, few in number; and there he became a nation, great, mighty, and populous. And the Egyptians treated us harshly, and afflicted us, and laid upon us hard bondage. Then we cried to the Lord the God of our fathers, and the Lord heard our voice, and saw our affliction, our toil, and our oppression; and the Lord brought us out of Egypt with a mighty hand and an outstretched arm, with great terror, with signs and wonders; and he brought us into this place and gave us this land, a land flowing with milk and honey. And behold, now I bring the first of the fruit of the ground, which thou, O Lord, hast given me'. And you shall set it down before the Lord your God; and you shall rejoice in all the good which the Lord your God has given to you and to your house, you, and the Levite, and the sojourner who is among you (Deut. 26.1–11).

Or notice how the sense of gratitude and trust, its acknowledgment
in word and expression in action, conveyed in this psalm:

> What shall I render to the Lord for all his bounty to me?
> I will lift up the cup of salvation and call on the name of the
>   Lord,
> I will pay my vows to the Lord in the presence of all his people.
> Precious in the sight of the Lord is the death of his saints.
> I Lord, I am thy servant; the son of thy handmaid.
> Thou hast loosed my bonds.
> I will offer to thee the sacrifice of thanksgiving and call on
>   the name of the Lord.
> I will pay my vows to the Lord in the presence of all his people,
>   in the courts of the Lord,
>   in your midst, O Jerusalem!
> Praise the Lord! (Ps. 116.12–19).

The Israelite, acknowledging in gratitude all that God has done
for him and his people, does so in word and act. He brings fruit,
raises a cup of wine, repeats the story. His faith is concretely and
publicly expressed in word, gesture and communal celebration
which includes feasting. The case for doing all this is not argued in
the Old Testament. It is assumed as natural.

So too with Paul, in the text (Rom. 10.9f.) quoted earlier. The
person says 'Jesus is Lord' because it is what he believes. And
because he believes it, he says it. 'No distinction is to be drawn
between the confession and the faith; the confession is believed
and the faith confessed' (C. K. Barrett).[1] Nor was this confession
likely to have been purely verbal. Quite probably, these were the
words which customarily accompanied the rite of baptism.

The Greek verb which Paul uses in Romans 10.9f., translated
by the English 'to confess' is *homologein*, and can have several
meanings in New Testament contexts. The basic meaning in this
instance appears to be to 'declare', 'profess', 'avow', 'proclaim'.
The believer declares how it is with himself and God. To say that
Jesus is Lord is a summary way of affirming one's faith that the
crucified Jesus is now exalted, that this is of God's doing, and
that the God who has so acted is utterly to be trusted for salvation. Another striking instance of Paul's view of the unity between faith and its confession is found in II Corinthians 4.13:
'Since we have the same spirit of faith as he had who wrote,

"I believed, and so I spoke," we too believe, and so we speak.'

This unity between faith and its confession, between its interior and exterior aspects, is not to be discarded as reflecting a primitive and outmoded view of man. Modern, Western man tends towards a sharp distinction between the 'inner man' with his thoughts, feelings and decisions, and his outward, bodily components. He may not believe as commonly as in former ages that he has an immortal soul, but he does tend to assume that he wears his body like a piece of clothing over his 'real self'. On such a view, one's inner life need not have any corresponding outward manifestation.

In fact, over wide areas of activity and experience we make nonsense of this 'ghost in a machine' view of ourselves. A moment's reflection teaches us how dependent we are on words, gestures, even facial expressions, for communicating our thoughts and feelings. A handshake, for instance, in our particular culture is a most significant gesture. To shake hands with someone to whom you have just been introduced, is to affirm to that person that you acknowledge their presence, accept them, and are at least prepared to be interested in them. Where the expected handshake is not given, embarrassment and even hurt can result for it signifies reserve, coldness, even rejection, no matter what is said verbally. Shaking hands, one might say, is a confession, in a most concrete way, of inner goodwill. The increasing current interest in 'body-language' is perhaps a sign that in the Western world we are beginning to recover a sense of the importance of outward and bodily expression, in gesture and symbol as well as in words, for our total existence as persons.

The importance of outward verbal and bodily expression runs deeper even than the need to communicate our thoughts and feelings to others. It is often a matter of finding out, for ourselves, what in fact we are thinking and feeling. I said in a previous chapter that one of our basic human needs is to find out 'who' we are, and part of this quest involves uncovering the confusion of feelings and thoughts, aims and hopes and fears, within us. But usually, we can only discover and cope with what is inside us, by bringing it out and putting it outside ourselves, whether by words or by other means. It is on this that so much pastoral counselling is based. In coping with grief, for example, no one but the particular grieving person knows exactly how he or she feels.

And the bereaved may not be prepared to face fully the fact of
their bereavement, repressing the emotions that are welling up.
The grief must be expressed if it is to be coped with. There
must be tears, and the admission of all that is really felt of sorrow,
guilt or anger. What is inwardly felt must be outwardly expressed
if healing is to come. In other situations of crisis or anxiety, the
inward state of the sufferer may be much more complex and con-
voluted, to himself no less than to others. He requires someone
to whom he can talk, and talk at length, about his problems and
anxieties. Help is given by a counsellor who listens, in an open
and sympathetic way which encourages the client to put into
words how he feels and sees the situation. Often, it is as the client
is enabled to put his situation and feelings into words, that for the
first time he begins to realize what his problem actually is, and
how it may be faced. What is inward becomes recognizable by
becoming outward. It becomes capable of being grasped and dealt
with. By expressing himself, the client comes to identify himself,
and to own himself and his need in a new way.

Nor is this true only of situations of crisis and suffering. The
great high moments of life, when joy floods the soul like a river
bursting its banks, demand outward expression for reasons closely
parallel to those for expressing suffering and anxiety. The news of
the baby's safe birth, the examination success, the longed-for
appointment won, requires to be told. Only when such joy, however deeply felt, is put into words does it become wholly real to
the one who feels it. Only as we hear ourselves say to another
'It's happened!', 'I've done it!' does the particular experience
come home to us, to be really owned by us as part of *our* story and
written into the narrative. For our lives are stories, in continuous
process of being written by ourselves. Celebrations of achievements
and anniversaries are more than excuses for conviviality, with much
eating and drinking. They are a way of marking and solidifying the
experiences of the events that are so important to us, and thus
enable us to build their significance into the pattern of our lives.

The deeper we are *im*pressed, the more we need to *ex*press.
Only as we put on the outside, in concrete act, gesture, words,
what is within, do we really recognize what in fact is within.
Human life is embodied life. The concrete is not to be despised in
favour of the abstract, nor the bodily in favour of the 'spiritual'.
This wholeness of our humanity is perhaps most profoundly seen

in our sexual relationships. Growth in love, trust and commitment between a man and a woman is a relationship involving their total selves, in which no single aspect of the person can be omitted without the whole relationship suffering in consequence. Physical love is the means by which partners express and confirm their acceptance of and commitment to each other, and is the most concrete statement of what each means to the other, summing up what the relationship has meant hitherto, and providing the basis for further growth. In general, we are right to suspect claims for a purely 'Platonic' relationship.

We may seem to have strayed some way from the believer and his faith in God. But the believer is as fully human in his faith as in any other aspect of his life, and if, as has been stated, the essence of faith is a basic re-orientation of the self towards trust in the grace of God, then we should not be surprised if such an *im*-pressive situation should require an *ex*pressive 'confession', a declaration in concrete word and act of 'how it is'. Only as the person puts his faith on the outside in a specific way does he truly come to see it, grasp it, identify himself with it and own it as really his, and build it into the ongoing story of his life – not as another incident in that life, but indeed its fundamental theme. It does in fact seem to be the case, pastorally speaking, that most people who come to a new-found Christian faith do feel the need of this, and actually want to confess it in an appropriate ordinance of initiation. Equally it has to be recognized that an over-emphasis on the rite itself at the expense of the faith which it is expressing, can act as a deterrent to a full and free acceptance of faith, and great pastoral sensitivity has to be exercised in this area.

In Christian tradition, the primary means of confessing faith initially, is baptism which comprises both act and word: the use of water and the utterance by the candidate of the words of faith, the earliest form of which, we have seen, was probably simply 'Jesus is Lord'. This is not the place to expand a full sacramental theology, or to discuss the pros and cons of infant or believer's baptism. As regards the former subject, we are looking in this book at the issue of faith which, it has to be recognized, does not comprehend the whole reality of the sacrament. As regards the debate about the pros and cons of infant baptism, suffice it to say that in ecumenical discussion there seems to be a growing consensus that baptism with water and personal declaration of faith do belong together, and that if these elements are separated in time (as in infant baptism, followed by confirmation later) they are nevertheless to be seen as parts of essentially one process. The strongest argument for infant baptism, apart from its long tradition of use in the church, is that it makes clear the prevenient grace of God which seeks us even before our response to him. The strongest argument for believer's baptism, apart from the case that it was the norm in New Testament times and even for a long while afterwards, is that it declares so clearly the nature of faith as identification with Christ in his death and trust in his risen power. This feature is of course most powerfully conveyed in baptism by total immersion, and, for a Baptist at least, it is difficult to visualize a more concrete way of bringing Paul's words to life: 'Do you not know that all of us who have been baptized into Christ Jesus were baptized into his death? We were buried therefore with him by baptism into death, so that as Christ was raised from the dead by the glory of the Father, we too might walk in newness of life' (Rom. 6.3f.). Such an act is often spoken of as a 'witness', and it certainly can make a powerful impression on those present, and has been known to challenge others to a like faith. But if it is a witness, it is first and foremost a witness to the baptismal candidate himself. In this act, he is making external and concrete what he has been growingly conscious of within, and in so doing he is putting himself totally, as a complete spiritual, mental and bodily being, into his decision of trust. He states openly 'I believe that Jesus Christ is Lord'. He hears his own words, realizes that they are indeed *his* words, follows them out into the publicity of the congregation who also hear them, and receives them back as truly his own. What he is prepared to say before others, truly confirms that this is his faith. In entering the water, he is expressing what his faith means in terms of dying. He literally has to let go of himself and entrust himself to the one baptizing him and to the water. Letting go of oneself is, as we have seen, at the heart of faith in God, and baptism is a most apt expression of this, the more so since water is associated at a deep level in the human mind with death (which it can cause) and birth (which it accompanies). The total baptismal experience, then, enables a confession of faith to be made, by which the believer is enabled to grasp and own his faith. Completely identified with his faith, he is liberated to live in its power.

Earlier in this chapter, we saw how vital is the role of the 'listener' in enabling a person to externalize in words and non-verbal ways what he is struggling with inside himself. In a parallel way, the fact that a confession of faith is, by definition, a 'public' declaration, is crucial. It is when we are acknowledged by others to be what we aspire to be, that we are most fully set free to fulfil those aspirations. This is but another facet of the relational character of human life which has been emphasized repeatedly in this book. Again, it is not just that the candidate who confesses his faith in baptism, or confirmation, or whatever other ordinance, is witnessing to these present that this is his faith. *They* are also witnessing to *him* that this is indeed the case, by their acknowledgment and acceptance of what he is doing. The recognition and affirmation of the community seals the identity of new believer in his faith. Here lies much of the significance of such physical gestures as the laying on of hands, or the right hand of fellowship, which may accompany the confession of faith and reception into the community of the church.

This brings us to another aspect of the significance of faith as confession, namely, Christian existence as communal. Again, this is not the place for developing a theology of the church. It has been said often enough that there is no such thing as a solitary Christian. It could be that at the moment there are dangers in some quarters of going to the other extreme and imposing an enforced 'groupiness' in church life, which does not sufficiently respect the need for a proper individuality and a certain private dimension to each person's life. But to be brought into a relationship of trust in the gracious God known through Jesus brings us into a new relationship with others, and most immediately with others who share that faith. Paul speaks of the 'household' of faith (Gal. 6.10), not to mention his profound image of the church as the body of Christ, with Christians as differentiated but integral members of it (I Cor. 12.12–31). Any human group, if it is to remain a viable and cohesive unit, requires some recognized basis for its membership and identity, some agreed norm of character and commitment by which members can accept each other as belonging to the group, and work together in fulfilling its aims. The basis of membership of the church is faith in God through Christ, and it is only appropriate, therefore, that membership of the church should be upon personal confession of the faith which is the basis of the life and purpose of that community. This is a powerful reason why rites of initiation should always take place in the context of the whole congregation gathered for worship. Not only does the congregation help to confirm the candidate in his faith by witnessing his confession, but the candidate in turn witnesses to the members of the community that what he is confessing is their faith also. Such occasions can be powerful and renewing reminders to the whole community as to where the basis of its Christian existence lies.

Confession as the making external, concrete and apprehensible of faith, is not however confined to baptism and Christian initiation. It is one element in what happens whenever the community gathers to celebrate the eucharist. 'For as often as you eat this bread and drink the cup, you proclaim the Lord's death until he comes' (I Cor. 12.26). There are many levels, theological and psychological, in the eucharist, and to remark on the aspect of faith does not exhaust its meaning by any means. But it is worth noting Paul's reference to 'proclaiming' Christ's death in the eating of the bread and drinking from the cup. Christians have sometimes puzzled over this, for notwithstanding John Wesley's description of the communion service as a 'converting ordinance', it has seemed strange to them that a liturgical act taking place within the church and witnessed largely if not wholly by believers, should be called a 'proclamation' – a term usually associated with the public declaration of the gospel to those as yet untouched by faith. But it is not only non-believers who need presenting with the gospel. If faith is to be continually sustained and renewed, it needs concrete confession as a regular thing no less than at the beginning in baptism. It needs symbolizing and crystallizing in an act which embodies God's gracious self-giving and man's trustful response as both fulfilled in the death of Jesus, which is recalled in the bread and the cup. To participate in the eucharist is to share, individually and corporately, in this action which, by making faith concrete, enables believers to identify with that faith again, to renew their faith as they confess it, to receive it as they see it as a table spread before them.

But it is not solely in sacramental or liturgical acts that the Christian tradition has emphasized the confession of faith. Those who maintained their faith despite opposition or persecution came in the course of time to be known as 'confessors'. More pointedly

still, the term 'witness' – *martyr* in the Greek New Testament –
gradually came to be used as the technical term for those who
confessed their faith in the most absolute sense, in the sacrifice of
their lives. In the case of such a martyr, what is symbolized in
baptism becomes literally true in terms of dying with Christ. But
between the symbolism of baptism and the literalism of martyrdom lies a whole range of possibilities for faith to be made concrete as confession in word and deed, and here we are verging on
the area of commitment to be dealt with in the next chapter.

So far, we have seen the basis of faith as confession as lying
within human nature itself as a unity of inner and outer, of consciousness and concrete expression, and in the communal nature
of Christian existence. But finally, it has to be said that faith as
confession is rooted most profoundly in the nature of God himself. Faith is trust in the gracious God: not a God who is simply
over there, a static Prime Mover, but the living and dynamic One
who moves himself towards us to be with us and for us in our
midst. His graciousness is not some unchanging idea floating
above our earthly existence and its turmoil. It comes to us in
concrete words and acts in the midst of this historical turmoil.
God, we might say, is One who expresses what is within him, by
externalizing his will in concrete actions. The very existence and
sustenance of the universe is the concrete manifestation of his will
in outflowing creativity:

> The heavens are telling the glory of God;
> and the firmament proclaims his handiwork.
> Day to day pours forth speech,
> and night to night declares knowledge (Ps. 19.1f.).

> By the word of the Lord the heavens were made,
> and all their host by the breath of his mouth (Ps. 33.6).

For what can be known about God is plain to them, because
God has shown it to them. Ever since the creation of the world
his invisible nature, namely, his eternal power and deity, has
been clearly perceived in the things that have been made (Rom.
1.19f.).

The very being of the world is the concrete confession by God of
his will as Creator. Moreover, for the prophets and psalmists of

Israel the actual historical experiences of weal and woe which beset their people were to be interpreted as God's speaking and acting-out of his purpose towards them as Judge and Saviour. God is as God does – on the plane of worldly history. The historical event *par excellence*, in the light of which all others were viewed, was the deliverance and exodus from Egypt, seen as God's gracious act for his people to whom he bound himself in covenant. Such a God could be expected repeatedly to confess his purpose in concrete, historical ways. Second Isaiah, towards the end of the exile in Babylon, and watching the rise of the Persian Cyrus to military dominance, declares:

> Who stirred up one from the east whom victory meets at
>   every step?
> He gives up nations before him, so that he tramples kings
>   under foot:
>   he makes them like dust with his sword,
>   like driven stubble with his bow.
> He pursues them and passes on safely,
>   by paths his feet have not trod.
> Who has performed and done this,
>   calling the generations from the beginning?
> I, the Lord, the first and with the last; I am he (Isa. 41.2–4).

God himself could never be seen by mortal man. Even his name could scarcely be uttered by human lips. But he was known as the One who brought up his people out of the land of bondage, and as such was always to be reckoned with in their ongoing history. This is the theological background to the coming of Jesus, as the one who consummates God's coming to his people, and the people's response to him. Jesus is the fullest concrete confession by God of his mind and purpose for mankind, and the fullest concrete human confession of trust in and loyalty to God. 'And the Word became *flesh* and dwelt among us, full of grace and truth; we have beheld his glory, glory as of the only Son from the Father . . . No one has ever seen God; the only Son, who is in the bosom of the Father, he has made him known' (John 1.14, 18). The divine confession and the human confession meet as one in the most concrete and absolute way possible, in the voluntary death on the cross. 'In this the love of God was made manifest among us, that God sent his only Son into the world, so that we might live through him. In this is love, not that we loved God but that he loved us and sent his Son to be the expiation of our sins' (I John 4.9f.). 'But God shows his love for us, in that while we were yet sinners Christ died for us' (Rom. 5.8).

In other words, God has made no secret of his love, nor has he preserved it within himself as some kind of 'attitude'. He has confessed it, made it external and concrete in creation and in history, in the fullest possible way. He is not as inward and 'spiritual' as we ourselves sometimes aspire to be. He confesses his grace outwardly and concretely, and the human grasp of his grace can be no less concrete and open if it is to be real. It is the centrality of Jesus for faith which makes this clear. As we have argued in chapter 4, faith is faith *with* Jesus, Jesus who is himself the one who confessed trust in God in the fullest way. Paul enjoins the young Timothy: 'Take hold of the eternal life to which you were called when you made the good confession in the presence of many witnesses. In the presence of God who gives life to all things, and of Jesus Christ who in the presence of Pontius Pilate made the good confession, I charge you to keep the commandment unstained and free from reproach until the appearing of our Lord Jesus Christ' (I Tim. 6.12–14). In face of Jesus and his confession, there can be no inward retreat of faith. It is as actual as wood and nails. This concrete nature of faith's confession is emphasized most of all in the First Letter of John. 'He who confesses the Son confesses the Father' (2.22). To confess Jesus as the Son includes a recognition of his actual bodily existence in history – that he has come 'in the flesh' (4.2) as against a purely spiritualized view of Jesus as a quasi-human being. 'This is he who came by water and blood, Jesus Christ, not with the water only but with the water and the blood. And the Spirit is the witness, because the Spirit is the truth. There are three witnesses, the Spirit, the water and the blood; and these three agree' (5.6–8). Jesus' ministry was attested by the Spirit with which he was endowed and which opens men's eyes to see the truth which he is, *and* by his earthly, human course. The one who was baptized in the water of the Jordan was a real human person, identifying himself with sinful humanity. The one who died on the cross died an actual human death, shedding real human blood. Water and blood accompany the Spirit's testimony when God confesses his love and (note their strong baptismal and eucharistic overtones) when man confesses his trust.

7

Faith as Commitment

Today, one of the most popular words used in connection with the Christian life is 'commitment'. We speak of 'committed Christians' to mean those who consciously and actively profess Christianity, as distinct from those whose attachment is vague or nominal, or hesitant. In evangelical circles particularly, the acceptance and confession of Christian faith is often termed 'committing oneself to Christ'. In fact for many people 'faith' and 'commitment' have virtually become synonymous, and in writing this book so far I myself have had to check the natural impulse to speak of 'commitment' a number of times. I have felt it important to avoid the term as far as possible hitherto, in order to emphasize the central and basic element of faith as *trust* in the gracious God. An over-eagerness to speak of commitment can obscure this most basic aspect of faith with its recognition of the priority of God's grace in his movement towards us, and of our debt to him even for the relationship of faith itself. It should be remembered that commitment itself is hardly a biblical word. That it is so often on our lips to a great extent reflects our social and cultural milieu. Our modern Western ethos puts a high value on human freedom and responsibility. In contrast to a fixed social order such as existed in the feudal ages, when people had an assigned place in the social system from birth till death, our modern outlook at least pays lip-service to the right to choice over wide areas of life including marriage, career, leisure interests, political outlook, religious beliefs and so on. Concomitant with choice goes the need to accept the consequence of making those choices and the effort to realize the goals set by those choices. Thus for instance, while marriage is still undergirded by a form of legal contract, a heavier emphasis is now placed on the element of voluntary self-commitment by each partner to the other. Where that commitment fails, society and the law now permit divorce more readily than previously. A rising divorce-rate indicates an increasing failure to sustain marriage as a commitment 'till death us do part', but it also carries the assumption that commitment *is* of the essence of marriage and that when commitment fails there is little point in continuing the relationship.

'Commitment' bears several layers of meaning acquired through the history of its usage. The Latin verb *committere* literally means 'to join with' or 'send with'. A message or gift borne by a messenger is sent with that person, and hence committed or entrusted to his charge. Correspondingly, the one to whom the message or gift is entrusted is 'committed' to delivering it as directed. To have a commitment is therefore to be joined with something other than oneself, resulting in an engagement which restricts one's total freedom of action. The messenger is not free to do what he likes with the message. He has to see that it arrives at its destination, and that is his commitment. A 'committee' is a group of people entrusted with certain items of business delegated to them. As that group, they are not free to spend their time together talking about whatever they wish. They have an agenda which determines and shapes their conversation and decisions. Their energies are directed towards a goal which they have accepted. (This is why we have an ambivalent attitude towards committees. To be appointed to one can be counted a privilege, a mark of esteem and status, which presumably is why some people enjoy sitting on as many as possible. But they also bind us in a certain way, and can lead to all kinds of frustrations which we did not choose, which is why others of us try to avoid them like the plague.)

To be committed, or to commit oneself, thus conveys two senses – that of entrusting oneself to the care or direction of another, and that of being directed towards a particular goal. What we have so far explored in this book has largely been faith as trust, which can be said to be a form of commitment in the former sense. To trust in God is to commit oneself to God for absolute security, for salvation, to hand oneself over to his grace. In this sense, the active verb 'to commit' is certainly found in the Bible. 'To God would I commit my cause' (Job 5.8); 'Father, into thy hands I commit my spirit' (Luke 23.46). But 'to commit oneself' in the second sense, and the noun 'commitment', are terms scarcely found even in recent translations of the Bible, and this perhaps is indicative of the peculiarly modern provenance of the word.

The fact is that the Bible already has a rich store of terms denoting faith as a reality which shapes one's existence in a particular way, and which directs towards a certain goal. Moreover, if 'commitment' in its modern sense refers primarily to the independent, free-choosing and self-directing individual, then it does not fully coincide with the biblical understanding of a faith as a *response* to God who has made the first move towards us and only in relationship with whom faith can live. But 'commitment' has become so much a part of our religious vocabulary that it would be pointless to expunge it, and provided that the second of the two senses referred to above is not dissociated from the first, it can still be highly useful.

Faith, we have seen, is personal trust in the gracious God known in Jesus. Moreover, the trust is entered into by decision, which is a response to God's offer. Even more strongly, we trust because we are *called* by God to trust him. We do not, as it were, see a God whom we think it might be worth our while to rely on, as a useful security. We are met by grace which is a summoning grace. The message comes with an imperative, as it did on the lips of Jesus himself: 'Repent, and believe in the gospel' (Mark 1.15). In chapter 4, we saw how the grace of God meets us as a 'compelling truth'. That is, when we believe we do so not just because we think it will serve our interests to accept it, but because it *deserves* acceptance as the most basic truth there is. 'The saying is sure and *worthy* of full acceptance, that Christ Jesus came into the world to save sinners' (I Tim. 1.15). In short, the decision of trust is at the same time a decision of *obedience* to what is seen as meriting acknowledgment in its own right as the truth concerning God and ourselves. Our view of faith must therefore be qualified as *obedient* trust in the gracious God. In totally surrendering and entrusting ourselves to God as disclosed in Jesus, we accept God on his terms, not on ours. It is out of this acknowledgment that commitment in the Christian sense emerges. Faith can be described as commitment in that, in accepting God on his own terms, we accord him the right to shape our lives and determine our goals.

Christian commitment, in the active sense, is obedience. And the obedience begins with faith itself.

Indeed, we find in the Bible a close link between faith in God and obedience to him, to the extent that faith is often described as obedience. Luke states: 'And the word of God increased; and the number of disciples multiplied greatly in Jerusalem, and a great many of the priests were *obedient* to the faith' (Acts 6.7). Paul describes the purpose of his apostolic mission as 'to bring about the *obedience of faith* for the sake of [Christ's] name among all the nations' (Rom. 1.5). He speaks about the revelation of God's hidden purpose 'to bring about the *obedience of faith*' (Rom. 16.26). So also in the First Letter of Peter, the dedication is to those 'chosen by God the Father and sanctified by the Spirit for *obedience* to Jesus Christ and for sprinkling with his blood' (I Peter 1.2). In Acts again, we find Peter stating before the high priest: 'And we are witnesses to these things, and so is the Holy Spirit whom God has given to those who *obey him*' (Acts 5.32). The writer to the Hebrews speaks of Christ as being 'the source of eternal salvation to those who *obey* him' (Heb. 5.9). In his letter to the Galatians, which we have already examined as expressing so cogently Paul's emphasis on the centrality of faith as trust, Paul asks rhetorically: 'You were running well: who hindered you from *obeying the truth*?' (Gal. 5.7). Finally, we may cite the ominous warning in I Peter: 'For the time has come for judgment to begin with the household of God; and if it begins with us, what will be the end of those who *do not obey the gospel of God*?' (I Peter 4.17).

In trusting God for salvation, we are obeying his call to trust. We are obediently committing ourselves into his keeping in accordance with his declared will to be our God. From this relationship to God of trusting obedience and obedient trust stems the active aspect of commitment: the readiness to do whatever else he wills us to do. In faith, we have totally let go of ourselves and abandoned ourselves to him, not only for security but also for direction. The very fact that he wills to bring us into relationship with himself demonstrates that he is a God with a purpose to accomplish, a goal to reach, and to commit oneself to him *ipso facto* means a commitment to accept those goals ourselves. Stated in the most general terms, the goal is that of reflecting his nature within the conditions of our humanity and the world. He who is utterly holy, self-giving, gracious love, wants us as his creatures to grow in corresponding self-giving, gracious humanity. To accept him as our God cannot be done without accepting this goal, *his* goal, for ourselves. We cannot have his grace without his purpose. The Saviour and the Lord are one and the same God.

Specifically Christian faith is faith in God 'through Jesus Christ our Lord'. Jesus is the fullest embodiment of God's grace, and the fullest embodiment of the response to that grace in obedient trust. As we have seen (chapter 4) our faith is therefore a faith 'with Jesus' in the relationship of sonship to God. Faith is identification with Jesus. He is the ground and enabler of our trust in God, and the pointer to the way in which our lives will be shaped in obedience to God's purpose. He who enables us to commit our lives in obedient trust in God's grace, also points us to how we are to commit our lives in trustful obedience to God's will and purpose. So Christian commitment is the acceptance of Jesus as the most basic concrete goal for what we are to become as persons. We are committed to him because we are identified with him. The most profound meaning of baptism, indeed, is that by faith we are made one with Christ in his death, his total renunciation of sin and absolute obedience to the Father, thereby dying to the old humanity and entering upon the new life in the Spirit of Christ. Christian commitment is the working out of all that this baptismal confession means for the total life of the believer, as identification with Jesus Christ. The confession is itself the first step along the road of actual obedience, and sets the direction taken by that road.

Just as faith cannot fight shy of concrete confession by retreating into some purely inner sanctuary of devotion, neither can its continuing commitment and obedience remain disembodied and shapeless as an undefined 'attitude'. The God who has committed himself so utterly, actively and concretely to us even to the cross, cannot be served without an equally concrete loyalty in response. In the Old Testament, the God who out of sheer grace chose a people to be his own, who in mercy rescued them from oppression in Egypt and faithfully guided them through the wilderness wanderings to the promised land, requires a response of loyalty in an equally specific way. In the first place, the people are to worship no other gods, and the worship of their one God must be genuine. Further, their dealings with each other as neighbours must reflect the way God has dealt with the whole people: the way of 'steadfast love', faithfulness, mercy and compassion. Among his people, who exist only by virtue of his grace and compassion, there can be no defamation of one by another, no cheating in business, no usury, no adultery, no murder, no covetousness. Compassion must be shown to the poor and orphaned, and precisely because the people were themselves delivered when they were oppressed migrants in Egypt, compassion must be shown towards the foreigner or 'sojourner' in the land. The call to commitment in right worship and right dealings with each other is summarized in the words: 'For I am the Lord your God; consecrate yourselves therefore, and be holy, for I am holy' (Lev. 11.44). To exist in a right relationship to God means doing that which reflects his nature as holy, just and merciful. 'He has shown you, O man, what is good; and what does the Lord require of you but to do justice, and to love kindness, and to walk humbly with your God?' (Micah 6.8). Jeremiah aimed the message with stunning accuracy at a materialistic and self-satisfied king:

> Woe to him who builds his house by unrighteousness, and his
> upper rooms by injustice;
> who makes his neighbour serve him for nothing, and does
> not give him his wages;
> who says, 'I will build myself a great house with spacious
> upper rooms',
> and cuts out windows for it, panelling it with cedar, and
> painting it with vermillion.
> Do you think you are a king because you compete in cedar?
> Did not your father eat and drink and do justice and
> righteousness?
> Then it was well with him.
> He judged the cause of the poor and needy; then it was well.
> *Is not this to know me,* says the Lord? (Jer. 22.13–16).

As for Jesus himself, he repeatedly astonished those around him by his unparalleled stress on God's love and mercy, embodied in his own friendship offered even to the most despicable and hardened 'sinners', and by his forthright call to share his own utter commitment to live as God wills. Most significant here is the prayer which Jesus taught his followers. Not that the items in this prayer are in themselves particularly original to Jesus, reflecting as they do his background of contemporary Jewish piety. But their

order is crucial for an understanding of his view of the oneness
between faith and obedience:

> Our Father who art in heaven,
> Hallowed be thy name,
> Thy kingdom come,
> Thy will be done,
>   On earth as it is in heaven.
> Give us this day our daily bread;
> And forgive us our debts,
>   As we also have forgiven our debtors;
> And lead us not into temptation,
>   But deliver us from evil (Matt. 6.9–14).

'Our Father' – this form of address, which Jesus made peculiarly
his own, wholly captures the relationship of faith to God: absolute trust in his grace and therewith an identification with all that
God wishes to be accomplished in us and in all his creation.
'Hallowed be thy name': this is the recognition that God is to be
worshipped and served for his own sake, in his own right and on
his own terms. 'Thy kingdom come, Thy will be done' is the
prayer that God's cause, his purpose, will be accomplished in its
totality, both through our actions conforming to his will and by
means far extending beyond our own capabilities. The petitions
that follow for daily sustenance, for forgiveness (concomitant
with our commitment to forgive others likewise), and for pre-
servation from the power of evil are thus significant only on this
prior basis of total trust in God and utter commitment to his
cause. Just how closely, in Jesus' eyes, trusting acceptance of
God's mercy and commitment to a corresponding merciful relationship to others belong together, is vividly seen in his parable
of the unmerciful servant. The servant, released by his royal
master from a vast debt, went away and demanded payment from
a fellow servant who owed him a sum trivial by comparison. 'And
in anger his lord delivered him to the jailers, till he should pay all
his debt. So also my heavenly Father will do to every one of you,
if you do not forgive your brother from your heart' (Matt. 18.34f.).

Jesus summarized the whole teaching of the law and the prophets in the two greatest commandments: 'You shall love the
Lord your God with all your heart, and with all your soul, and
with all your strength, and with all your mind; and your neigh-

bour as yourself' (Luke 10.27). That is the commitment of those who live before God, and as Jesus showed in the story of the Good Samaritan, this is no abstract ideal, but a specific requirement which can meet us in any human encounter. But neither can this commitment be exhaustively set out and codified in a series of minutely defined 'laws' to cover every possible eventuality in advance. This was what some of the scribes and pharisees attempted to do. Not only is it quite unrealistic in face of life which continually surprises us with unforeseen circumstances, but, in Jesus' eyes, such a legalistic scheme hinders a true and full response to God. If right conduct is defined in an absolute and detailed way, it leads either to ridiculous and impossible burdens imposed upon people (in Sabbath observance, for example) or to a calculating attitude which seeks to get away with the *minimum* requirement of obedience, at least cost to oneself. Jesus' Sermon on the Mount is not a new legal code of injunctions on how to live a moral life. Its graphic sayings are pointers to the direction taken by a life grounded in trusting God's love and reflecting that love. Such a life will be a very concrete affair, but at the same time will always be bursting through the straitjacket of a legalistic code. Hence: love your enemies, not just your friends; give your cloak as well as your coat; go two miles, not just one. 'You, therefore, must be perfect, as your heavenly Father is perfect' (Matt. 5.48). Perfection here cannot be understood in terms of some legal standard of morality, a kind of marks scheme for doing good, but as a single-minded dedication to showing unreserved love in whatever situation it is called for. The rich man who came to Jesus enquiring what he must do to win 'eternal life' was puzzled because, on such a legalistic assessment of his life, he seemed to be perfect. But when Jesus faced him with the command to give away all he owned to the poor, and literally to follow him, he could not. He was too committed to his own moral perfection as well as his 'great possessions', to take a concrete step of obedience to God's cause, a step which in his case would have truly reflected God's kingdom – selfless giving to others in their need. The kingdom is like a pearl of great price, worth giving up everything else for its sake.

So Jesus, in his own words, came not to 'abolish the law and the prophets' but to fulfil them – that is, to bring out to the fullest possible extent the nature of commitment to God as concrete, obedient response to his love. To believe in God through Jesus, to identify with Jesus, therefore means a commitment to opening our lives as unreservedly as possible to the way of love which Jesus taught and exemplified all the way to the cross. That cross, where Jesus gave himself totally for God's cause and his people's redemption, is at once the embodiment of the mercy in which we trust, and the marker of our true humanity.

The nature of faith as obedient trust and trusting obedience has nowhere in modern times been more clearly expounded than by Dietrich Bonhoeffer in his classic *The Cost of Discipleship*. 'Only those who obey can believe, and only those who believe can obey.'[1] The book was written during Bonhoeffer's involvement in the German Church struggle, while he was in charge of an illegal seminary of the Confessing Church. At a time when it was all too easy for Christians to retreat into a religious ghetto and close their eyes to what was happening in their society, the book represented a summons to concrete obedience to the command of Christ as indissolubly bound up with faith. Otherwise grace became 'cheap grace', a complacent acquiescence in the thought of God's goodness, confusing mercy with indulgence, instead of 'costly grace' which involves an actual following of Jesus with all the risks of suffering with him. Bonhoeffer writes:

> The actual call of Jesus and the response of single-minded obedience have an irrevocable significance. By means of them Jesus calls people into an actual situation where faith is possible. For that reason his call is an actual call and he wishes it so to be understood, because he knows that it is only through actual obedience that a man can become liberated to believe.[2]

In Nazi Germany, whether one truly trusted in God was a question that could not be answered simply in terms of inward devotion or adherence to the orthodox creeds of the church. The question was posed in terms of one's response to militarism and state-worship, the suppression of truth and the oppression of the Jews. One could not claim to believe in God and at the same time pass by such blatant contradictions of God's will and purpose as known in Jesus Christ. To refuse to do what God requires is, in effect, to deny that God really stands before us with his claim upon us. We cannot put our faith in God with one hand, while with the other we push him out of our real existence.

The unity of faith and obedient action can be expressed another way. In doing what we understand to be God's will, that will is not to be viewed as some kind of directive which he has issued and which now exists as an entity by itself, rather like an Act of Parliament which can remain in force and on the Statute Book long after that particular Parliament has been dissolved. God's will is an expression of his very nature. We are committed to a life of love and service because God himself is love, not simply because he has told us to love. It is the natural and appropriate way of life for those who now have the 'Abba!' type of relationship to him, as children of the Father who is ceaselessly and inexhaustibly active in creative and redemptive love. An act of loving service, a movement of creative sacrifice, a protest against injustice, an enabling of reconciliation – such commitments are entered into not because they conform to some code of behaviour labelled 'God's will', but because these express how God himself is regarding that situation, and indeed, through his Spirit, involved in that situation. To enter into such commitments is to confess in the most concrete way who we believe God is, and what the deepest truth about that situation is. Or, as put most succinctly in the New Testament:

Whoever confesses that Jesus is the Son of God, God abides in him, and he in God. So we know and believe the love God has for us. God is love, and he who abides in love abides in God, and God abides in him. In this is love perfected with us, that we may have confidence for the day of judgment, because as he is so are we in this world. There is no fear in love, but perfect love casts out fear. For fear has to do with punishment, and he who fears is not perfected in love. We love, because he first loved us. If anyone says, 'I love God', and hates his brother, he is a liar; for he who does not love his brother whom he has seen, cannot love God whom he has not seen. And this commandment we have from him, that he who loves God should love his brother also (I John 4.13–21).

'As he is, so are we in this world'; that is the heart of the matter. Faith is a unity in relationship with God by trust in his grace, and that unity in relationship – an 'abiding in God' – is owned and made concrete by confession and commitment to love as he loves. Thus faith moves naturally into *faithfulness*, a steadfast, loyal adherence to doing what God wills of us, and at times an enduring of what he wills us to suffer. It is such faithfulness which is given such great prominence throughout the Old Testament, and most especially, as A. R. Johnson shows in his recent monumental study of the psalms, in Hebrew worship.[3] The chosen nation, and members of it, are to live righteous lives with a consistency corresponding to God's unrelenting steadfast love towards them, for 'all his work is done in faithfulness' (Ps. 33.4). Indeed, as we have seen, the 'faith' by which the 'righteous' shall live referred to in Habakkuk 2.4 could well in the original Hebrew carry this nuance of 'faithfulness' or 'steadfast loyalty' rather than sheer 'trust'.[4] But, as we have also seen, 'faith' as trust is also deeply embedded in the Old Testament, and it would be quite unwarranted to set 'faith' and 'faithfulness' over against each other. The latter is borne out of the former, and the former survives so long as it is expressed in the latter.

Because faith has this double aspect of passive trust and active faithfulness, of commital of oneself into the care of God and commitment to do what he requires, it is not surprising that almost from the beginning of Christianity there has been a tendency at times to separate them and set them in opposition, seeing them as independent possibilities instead of poles of one indivisible whole. This is of course the hoary old issue of 'justification by faith' versus 'justification by works'. Fuel for the controversy can be found even in the New Testament itself, notably the Letter of James:

What does it profit, my brethren, if a man says he has faith but has not works? Can his faith save him? If a brother or sister is ill-clad and in lack of daily food, and one of you says to them, 'Go in peace, be warmed and filled', without giving them the things needed for the body, what does it profit? So faith by itself, if it has no works, is dead. But some one will say, 'You have faith and I have works'. Show me your faith apart from your works, and I by my works will show you my faith. You believe that God is one; you do well. Even the demons believe – and shudder. Do you want to be shown, you foolish fellow, that faith apart from works is barren? Was not Abraham our Father justified by works, when he offered his son Isaac upon the altar? You see that faith was active along with his works, and faith was completed by works, and the scripture was fulfilled which says, 'Abraham believed God, and it was reckoned to him as righteousness'; and he was called the friend of God. You see that a man was justified by works and not by faith alone. And in the same way was not also Rahab the prostitute justified by works when she received the messengers and sent them out another way? For as the body apart from the spirit is dead, so faith apart from works is dead (James 2.14–26).

It is a matter of scholarly debate whether James was explicitly attacking the teaching of Paul, but it is not difficult to imagine how a bowdlerized version of Paul's views circulating in the early church would draw the kind of fire dispatched in this passage. Paul, for his part, strove to refute any notion that salvation by grace through faith obviated the need for moral commitment, as vigorously as he rejected the idea that moral effort could by itself justify the sinner.

How can we who died to sin still live in it? Do you not know that all of us who have been baptized into Christ Jesus were baptized into his death? We were buried therefore with him by baptism into death, so that as Christ was raised from the dead by the glory of the Father, we too might walk in newness of life (Rom. 6.1–4).

Let not sin therefore reign in your mortal bodies, to make you obey their passions. Do not yield your members to sin as instruments of wickedness, but yield yourselves to God as men who have been brought from death to life, and your members to God as instruments of righteousness (Rom. 6.12f.).

The merest glance at Paul's letters shows how much attention he gave to Christian ethical behaviour, to the concrete shape and direction fitting for those who live in relationship to God through Christ. Those who commit themselves to the grace and mercy of God, thereby also commit themselves to fulfilling his requirements:

I appeal to you, therefore, brethren, by the mercies of God, to present your bodies as a living sacrifice, holy and acceptable to God, which in your spiritual worship. Do not be conformed to this world but be transformed by the renewal of your mind, that you may prove what is the will of God, what is good and acceptable and perfect (Rom. 12.1f.).

If we can imagine Paul in conversation with James (and a lively exchange it would undoubtedly have been), Paul would have stuck to his bedrock belief that as far as our saving relationship to God is concerned, it *is* a matter of trustful acceptance of God's grace seen in the crucified and risen Jesus. But he would have gone along with James that such a relationship 'without works is dead', or, in his own words what matters is 'faith working through love' (Gal. 5.7). But it is *faith* which is active. Luther too, who in a well-known phrase called the Letter of James a 'thing of straw', stressed the activity of faith, and could say:

> O, it is a living, busy, active, mighty thing, this faith; and so it is impossible for it not to do good works incessantly . . . Hence a man is ready and glad, without compulsion, to do good to everyone, to suffer everything, in love and praise of God, who has shown him this grace; and thus it is impossible to separate works from faith, quite as impossible as to separate heat and light from fire.[5]

The fact that faith means both trust and commitment should deter us from seeking to impose a single, uniform route to full acceptance of the Lordship of Christ. This needs to be borne in mind in evangelism, pastoral care and in the education provided by the community of the church. Chronologically speaking, for some people the decision of faith as trust is the primary stage. The ground is crumbling in confusion under one's feet. Where all else is proving insecure, the grace of God is grasped as the one absolute security. Christ comes as God-for-us, the very present help in trouble. For others, Christ appears initially as the challenging and inspiring Man-for-others. In a world of private selfishness and public power-seeking, there is a stirring of the spirit at the sight of one giving himself in love to others to the point of the cross. That vision may most effectively be conveyed by another life touched by the same spirit, a Mother Teresa or the quiet neighbour down the road who so genuinely cares and is happy in caring, whether rewarded or not. At one extreme, faith may come as the response to the call to entrust oneself to God. At the other, it may begin with the vision of what it could mean for a one-third overfed and two-thirds starving world, to put on the new humanity of Christ. But from whichever pole the start is made, there must be movement towards the other pole. Whoever grasps God in sheer trust will sooner or later know the challenge to give as freely as he or she has received. And whoever would set out to join with God in renewing the earth, will sooner or later realize that we can only love because of him who first loved us, and that the only secure ground for our actions lies beyond ourselves, in the grace of God.

Faith, then, means commitment: being joined with the cause and purpose of God whose grace we trust, a trusting obedience and an obedient trust. God has declared and consummated his cause and purpose in Jesus Christ as the means of grace and the pattern of life. To believe therefore means putting oneself at the disposal of God as he seeks to bring all his children and all his creation into his love as disclosed in Christ. In faith, therefore, one is no longer one's own master. In the superb words of the Methodist Covenant Service:

> I am no longer my own, but Thine. Put me to what Thou wilt, rank me with whom Thou wilt; put me to doing, put me to suffering; let me be employed for Thee or laid aside for Thee, exalted for Thee or brought low for Thee; let me be full, let me be empty; let me have all things, let me have nothing; I freely and heartily yield all things to Thy pleasure and disposal.

The absolute commitment of the Christian is to Jesus Christ himself, confessed in baptism, continually recalled in the eucharist, apprehended in prayer and contemplation, and witnessed to in the worship and service of the community of the church. The believer is one who does not shrink from identification with the name of Jesus, and who joyfully shares in the honouring and proclamation of that name through the church, through the concrete decisions of life, and in the ordering of the society in which he or she lives. The relationship to God in Christ extends its commitment over the whole range of life. Christ being God's saving truth, and God being the Creator and Sustainer of all that is, there can be nothing which is not material for commitment to him. Personal behaviour and relationships with others, the stewardship of time and money, the responsibilities of home and family life, civic and political responsibilities: to be committed to God in Christ means to seek and to discern and obey his purpose in these and every other sphere. That sounds like a tall order, and it is. Once we widen our focus from the absoluteness of commitment to Christ himself, the issues of concrete obedience become less clear-cut. What are

'Christian standards' in sexual morality today? Should Christians press for unilateral nuclear disarmament? Is a just order in society to be equated with a thoroughly socialist system, or a moderated capitalism, or what? Because of the ambiguities and complexities of many of the issues in society today, any concrete commitment on which we embark is bound to seem relative and provisional in comparison with our absolute commitment to Christ himself. Christ cannot finally be identified with any social or political programme, or indeed any accepted ethos of moral behaviour. But neither can Christ be served in a vacuum, in abstraction from our social, cultural and political matrix. Those who complain about the 'politicization' of Christianity by, for example, the World Council of Churches, would do well to examine their own 'pure gospel' or 'spiritual' idea of salvation for hidden assumptions of vast political import. A wholly inward, privatized and individual religion is tailor-made for totalitarianism. That a wider commitment to justice and human dignity may lead us into grey areas of engagement is therefore insufficient reason to eschew it. Indeed, precisely through our absolute hold on God in Christ, or rather the sense of his absolute hold upon us, we should have the courage to step out on to the shifting waves of a hazardous sea of troubles, even if we cannot be one hundred per cent certain of the outcome. John Taylor is scarcely too provocative: 'To choose is to commit yourself. To commit yourself is to run the risk of failure, the risk of sin, the risk of betrayal. Jesus can deal with all those, for forgiveness is his metier. The only thing he can do nothing with is the refusal to be committed. Even Judas should do quickly whatever he chooses to do and be responsible.'[6] Equally, that absolute hold on God, which recognizes that he alone is all truth and goodness, should give us the humility to recognize that at the end of the day even our deepest insights and most splendid acts will need his correction and forgiveness. Herbert Butterfield's now famous aphorism is perhaps too simplistic: 'Hold to Christ and for the rest be totally uncommitted.'[7] We might more truthfully say 'Hold absolutely to Christ, and for the rest be relatively committed'. The trouble is that for a lot of the time we are not even relatively committed and, more than we dare admit, many of our so-called doubts and uncertainties about faith are a rationalizing of our unwillingness to let go, to step out, to risk and be vulnerable.

8

Faith as Freedom

If faith is a relationship of personal trust in the gracious God, entered into by decision, made concrete by confession and maintained in the commitment of service, it is also from beginning to end characterized by freedom. Admittedly, this has not always appeared so in the story of Christianity. All too often, 'having a faith' has appeared to mean being mentally lumbered with a burden of dogmas and doctrines to be accepted on the authority of the church or the Bible, and being imprisoned within a strait-jacket of rigid moral codes. Indeed, if, as stated in the previous chapter, faith means commitment, does not that mean a severe limitation on freedom? For being committed to – bound to – a person, a belief, or a particular way of life, we have from that point on excluded certain options for ourselves.

At this point, the discussion is in danger of stalling and spinning into that fatal dive which is the end of so many arguments about freedom. No word is more cherished, unless it is the more emotive term 'liberty'. Yet when we try to pin it down by asking, for example, 'How free are we?', it tends to become so rarified that we wonder if it has any content at all. In the face of all those features of our lives in which we have no choice and which we cannot change, is freedom any more than a dream? We may say that freedom is basically the capacity of choice, of self-determination, or the capacity to be the 'I' that I am, so as to fulfil my most cherished hopes and values. Yet when all is said and done, the 'I' that is me is to a great extent given. I cannot really turn myself into another 'I'. I have to live with myself to the end. Taken to its logical conclusion, is not this the ultimate denial of any freedom?

The discussion can be landed safely only when it is recognized that 'freedom' cannot be understood in abstraction, as though it were some kind of entity which could be lifted out of the specific contexts in which it operates, for the purposes of examination. On the social and political level it is this abstract approach which bedevils so much debate about freedom in different parts of the world. To a Westerner, freedom may be seen primarily in terms of the individual's right and ability to make choices for himself regarding personal behaviour, career, political and religious belief and so forth. To a Marxist in Eastern Europe, freedom may be seen primarily as the capacity of the people collectively, to progress towards greater material prosperity independently of market forces. To a citizen of a third world country, freedom may be primarily a matter of liberation from poverty and colonial oppression. At once, it is seen that freedom only means anything at all when we know *whose* freedom we are talking about, what we are supposed to be free *from*, and what *for*.

Freedom requires a particular context. The French airman and writer Exupéry tells a story about an African who was captured and enslaved by Arabs in the Sahara. After many years of slavery at a desert trading post, several French pilots clubbed together and bought him his release, then flew him to a city from where he could easily return home. He spent all day wandering round the city, enjoying (so he first thought) his new found freedom in the bars and cafés. But a few hours of self-indulgence left him disillusioned, for he was still utterly alone. So he went to the bazaar, buying whatever he could afford in the way of sweets and trinkets. These he gave away to the crowds of children begging in the street. At least, he now had friends of a sort. He had found that he could not be truly free, unless he had others with whom he could be free.

Truly human life, as has been argued earlier in this book, is life in relationships. Relationships are the basis of human existence, and it is therefore only as a factor in relationships that 'freedom' acquires any worth. The freedom to do just what I like with myself proves to be no freedom at all, and ends in a cul-de-sac of isolation. It is precisely when I recognize the part that others can and should play in my life that new possibilities open up for my growth as a person. A real friendship involves commitment, a certain tying down of myself. At the same time, friends are those who enable us to say and do things impossible on our own.

The freedom of faith must likewise be seen in its own peculiar context. Faith is the trusting and obedient relationship to the gracious God apprehended in Jesus Christ. God offers and summons. Man responds in trust. The relationship is entered into by human decision and yet is of God's gracious initiative, a 'unity in relationship' between the believer and the Giver. From the human side the decision is free, yet it is a freedom which recognizes that it can do no other in face of the utter truth which it sees. That is, it is a freedom which is not an arbitrary, self-willed choice, but a choice to respond to what fully merits acceptance. One recalls the words of Isaac Watts' famous hymn:

> Love so amazing, so divine,
> *Demands* my life, my soul, my all.

Faith is thus freedom in relationship to God. There is nothing between the believer and God, for the relationship is compounded of God's free grace and man's utter trust. It is the freedom, initiated and enabled by God, to relate to God without let or hindrance by any other factor. In Paul's language, it is the freedom of being in relation to God as a child to his father, as distinct from the relationship of a slave to his master:

> . . . when the time had fully come, God sent forth his Son, born of woman, born under the law, to redeem those who were under the law, so that we might receive adoption as sons. And because you are sons, God has sent the Spirit of his Son into our hearts, crying 'Abba! Father!' So through God you are no longer a slave but a son, and if a son then an heir (Gal. 4.4–7).

A slave or servant relates to his owner and master in a less than direct, personal way. It is a matter of duty. The slave relates to the orders for the day, rather than to the master himself as a person. His existence is one of obedience to orders, and he can expect no more than a basic minimum of just treatment or wages in return. His relationship to his master is determined by the measure of his obedience, and hence he can only feel secure in the presence of his master in so far as his obedience justifies approval. The son, however, has the free and intimate relation with the master as his father, whose direct love and care he now receives, and whose property he will one day inherit. Obedience will still be expected, not in order that the child may become a son, but because he is one, by blood or adoption. The relationship is natural and spontaneous, neither needing nor allowing any legalistic considerations to obtrude.

The freedom of faith is thus the freedom which God himself grants us to relate to him in trust and obedience, a relationship which is independent of all considerations outside God's grace and our trust. As in all relationships of a truly personal kind, there is an element of mystery which eludes exact analysis. It cannot be exactly explained, yet it can be expressed in the spontaneous, child-like address 'Abba!'. But in Christian terms, the freedom of faith can be theologically stated as consisting of a sharing in the freedom which Jesus himself demonstrated through his own utterly trusting and obedient self-giving to his Father. In face of the cross where God consummates his graciousness towards us, and where the human response is fulfilled in Jesus, faith knows that it is free to go to God, however empty its hand may be. The freedom of faith is the freedom to live with God and for God, by virtue of his love which invites and summons our trust.

But this basic freedom of faith requires to be spelled out further in its implications. The basic context of the freedom which is faith, is simply the relation between God and the believer. But the believer is a person set in a multitude of relationships in his world. How does the freedom of his relationship to God bear on his interactions with other persons, with his society and the world around him, and not least with himself? From what, and for what, is the believer free in these relationships? I would suggest five ways in which the freedom of faith is manifest in the totality of life.

First, faith means *freedom from self-concern and freedom for self-acceptance*. Much of our energy is directed at trying to build a basic security for ourselves, often regardless of or at the expense of others. Such an effort to live a life independently of God and others is, in traditional language, sin. Such a life is caught in a vicious spiral of concern for ourselves. The concern may be manifested in a never-ending search for material possessions, in the hope that these may somehow guarantee us a lasting sense of worthwhileness and satisfaction. Our 'being', we know, is an uncertain thing, so maybe it can be bolstered by a greater degree of 'having', as though what we own is an extension and enlargement of ourselves. The acquisitive individual, and the acquisitive society, are pointed up by Jesus in his parable of the rich man who tragically took security in extending his barns. 'And I will say to my soul, Soul, you have ample goods laid up for many years; take your ease, eat, drink, be merry' (Luke 12.19). Or the effort at enlargement may take the form of ambitions for status, recognition or power for oneself (or one's children). But self-concern has other and perhaps more common manifestations than such forms of greed. Living and growing are a rough-and-tumble business, with many knocks and bruises on the way. Self-concern may be manifested as a certain timidity, a refusal to take decisions, an evasion of responsibilities, a readiness to pass the buck to others and to blame 'them' when things go wrong. We would like to ensure ourselves against criticism and failure by hiding behind others, or by always looking for a 'strong lead' from someone else. The big wide world is a risky place, so stay at home and do nothing – after all, modesty is a virtue, is it not? Self-concern has still other guises. Self-criticism, Dr Johnson noted, can be the highest form of self-praise, since by it a man would show us how much he has to spare. But still more revealing about our attitudes to ourselves, is the angry criticism we indulge in against certain other people, which is often a projection of our dislike and fear of the same objectionable traits in ourselves. Subconsciously we know we are not as we should be, and that there are dubious facets to our personalities. But we do not know how to handle them without tearing ourselves apart and so we (note the phrase) 'take it out' on others.

Faith, being the glad acceptance of God's love for us, knows the strange and well-nigh baffling experience of being accepted and forgiven by God, despite all that we are. We come knowing we barely deserve to be called his hired servants, yet he welcomes us home as long-lost children, and kills the fatted calf. There is no longer any need to pretend that we are other than we are. No longer any cause to try to add a cubit to our stature by anxiety and feverish effort. We can accept ourselves and live with ourselves, because we know God accepts us and wants to live with us. Pious self-criticism and intolerance of others' quirks alike become irrelevant. We can, in the truest sense of the word, enjoy ourselves, and others too. In face of God's grace, we know that there is an essential humour about our situation. We have found the only certain security there can ever be, and on that basis we are freed from the drive to enlarge ourselves, protect ourselves, praise ourselves or morbidly condemn ourselves, for we now begin to see ourselves as God sees us. Not that our genuine wants and faults become any less real. Indeed, we are now in a position to face the uglier truth about ourselves more openly and honestly than ever. But now we know that all we can be and hope to be lies not in our hands alone, but in God's.

Second, faith brings *freedom from captivity to the past and freedom for openness to the future*. As human beings, we are unavoidably and deeply conscious of *time*. We are conscious of today, but are also full of remembrances of our yesterdays, and of hopes and fears about our tomorrows, and these affect each other deeply while at the same time greatly influencing how we live at the present moment. We are essentially forward-looking creatures. The first of our ancestors who planted a young sapling was marking a momentous step in the advance to recognizable humanity. But what we anticipate is to a great extent wrought out of our experience hitherto. That of course is what makes a human life purposeful. In dealing with the problems facing me in the coming week, I consciously and unconsciously draw upon my experience of similar occasions, and of how I and others behaved then. It is an illusion that the past is over and done with. So often, it is very much with us still, and should be. As Karl Jaspers said after the horrors of the Second World War, those who forget the past will have to relive it. But the presence of the past, as well as guiding, correcting and enriching, can also make life fearful. Most especially, in an individual's life, the past can pursue the present as the miasma of guilt. The past failure, the broken relationship, the evaded responsibility, may have occurred years ago, may scarcely even be consciously recalled. But it still eats away at us. Well did Keats appeal to sleep to

> Save me from curious conscience, that still lords
> Its strength for darkness, burrowing like a mole.

The past failure can persistently drag us back, making us look at it again and again, while all the time we are helpless to put it to rights since 'What's done cannot be undone'. Or, the past can keep us looking back over our shoulder, whispering 'If only . . .'. If only we had chosen a different career, or studied a different subject, or married a different partner . . . things would be different now. Or perhaps the past continues to beguile us because, in contrast to the cares and frustrations of the present, it seems like a beautiful dream-land where there were no problems, no crises, no fears. So we nostalgically dream of childhood again, or college days, or the job we were in before this one, and wish we were back there. This particular form of captivity to the past can of course beset not only individuals, but whole communities. The nation which has lost an empire and still has to find a role in the world, the church which remembers the good old days when Sunday worship was the social norm, can be tempted to wish for a future only as an unrealistic restoration of what once was (or imagined to have been). One way or another, the past can captivate us – either by its fearfulness which will not let us face the present and its creative opportunities, or by its seductive attractiveness which offers an escape from the present and its challenges.

Faith releases us from such spells, in order to face the future responsibly and hopefully. Whatever may be the truth, ugly or beautiful, about our past, faith knows that God has entered in by his grace and claimed us for his own to live freely in the relation of sonship to him. That God has met us so graciously, and that we now have free access to him who shapes all things, is now the great fact of our existence in view of which we have a new future. In Paul's terminology, to be by faith a son of God is to be an *heir* of God, that is, someone who can live in *expectation* of the wealth of future possibilities with which God can endow our existence. Our past is not disowned or wiped totally from memory. But it is taken, sins and all, into God's forgiveness. It is no longer our own burden, but it is assumed by God as his too. In adopting our past as his care, he offers us his future purpose as our hope. The crucifixion of Jesus was a summing-up of all the sinful self-assertion and vanity in human history. But it was also the summing up by God of his forgiving grace. Left to itself, human history runs out in futility, guilt and death. But it is not left to itself. It is not chained to the past in hopelessness. It is taken up into God himself, and in relationship to God we are free to look forward with him. 'May the God of hope fill you with all joy and peace in believing, so that by the power of the Holy Spirit you may abound in hope' (Rom. 15.13). Our personal history and the history of our world is therefore now a history with all kinds of new possibilities of fulfilment. The freedom of faith issues in new imagination, new quests, new ventures in understanding and living, new frontiers to be explored in what it means to be human in God's world.

But what of death, the stark end to life as we know it? The existentialist philosopher Martin Heidegger saw the awareness of death as the clue to human existence. So much of human life is caught up in anxiety in face of this, our 'ownmost possibility'. Authentic existence, according to Heidegger, lies in facing the inevitability and absoluteness of death in 'anticipatory resoluteness'.[1] In full acceptance of it, we are free to take responsibility for ourselves here and now. This is a courageous and open-eyed attitude, and it cannot be doubted that many people who have not believed in God have nevertheless been able to accept the inevitability and finality of their death with a humble contentment, grateful for the life that has been.

Faith is free to face death: not, however, because it sees death as the final limit to our existence. For faith, death is not the final limit to our existence, but the last frontier that we can at present glimpse. Death must be recognized, but not idolized. Not death, but *God*, is the One who stands absolutely over against us as the One with whom we ultimately have to do. But because faith, the relationship of sonship to God, knows that this God in his grace is *absolutely for us*, it knows that nothing else is ultimately to be feared, not even death. He who has accepted our past and comes to us in our present, will be our God for ever. Our future, even our death, can be entrusted to him no less than our present and our past. God is now our future. He who vindicated the crucified Jesus and made him known as the living one, can be trusted to take care of us and fulfil his purpose in us, in life, in death and whatever lies beyond. The God whose grace proves utterly realiable when we let go of ourselves to trust him, will be the same when we have to let go of this existence as we know it. Indeed, as we have seen, the decision of faith is a kind of death leading to new life. Dying is not simply something to be faced in 'anticipatory resoluteness', but is already built into the life and experience of the believer, from baptism onwards. Because faith is existence which has already 'passed out of death into life' (I John 3.14), it is free to embrace whatever forms death may assume in the future.

Third, the freedom of faith is *freedom from legalism and moralism and freedom for truly lawful and moral living*. Human society requires a substantial consensus of moral codes and enforceable laws if life is not to be anarchic. Codes, rules and laws are necessary: it is as simple as that. Further, as we have seen, the commitment of faith includes the commitment of obedience to fulfilling what is known of God's will and purpose for human life. Faith does not mean antinomianism. There is however a big difference between living in accordance with the law and moral codes in recognition of their role in sustaining community, on the one hand, and on the other hand living legalistically and moralistically. To live legalistically is to see the law as the be-all and end-all of existence. To live moralistically is to assess and judge human behaviour purely in terms of its conformity to some moral code as an absolute standard.

The legalistic attitude sees the law as something existing in its own right and possessing absolute validity, independent of its basic purpose which is to make social life tolerable for all. It becomes regarded as a power and authority on its own, an external straitjacket demanding conformity come what may. An extreme example today would be the attitude of some religious groups to certain of the archaic laws on Sunday observance. Although such laws were framed in the social and cultural climate of a very different age, and are regarded by the vast majority today as irrelevant and unwarrantably restrictive (on the odd occasions when they are enforced), an effort is still made to impose them. Legalism fails to recognize that times and circumstances change, and that the law must relate realistically to the society for which they are intended. Of greater import, at the present time, is the issue of whether some of our most prominent organizations working for overseas aid are extending their activities beyond the strict limits of the laws relating to 'charities' – many of which date from Elizabethan times.

In turn, the moralistic attitude sees the prime question in each situation as, 'Has this person offended against the moral code?' So, for example, unmarried mothers, and even the unemployed, as well as convicts, are regarded simply as defaulters rather than as people who also have acute problems. People are here primarily to be 'good' (which usually means, 'like ourselves') and to be judged accordingly.

To see codes of behaviour, whether enshrined in the Statute Book or otherwise, in such an absolute way is to hand over our responsibility as persons to an external, impersonal system governing our conduct. We are then on the way to becoming automatons instead of responsible beings making conscious choices. Moreover, when the law or moral code is made so central, it tends to become the *minimum* measure of a 'good life', and the fact that *we* have never appeared in court, or had an illicit affair, breeds a complacent moral self-satisfaction which spiritually can be as dangerous as flouting the law. Particularly when the codes are given religious sanction, legalism and moralism become most menacing, for they become determinative of the way we see ourselves in relation to God. Relating to God is equated with conformity to an external norm of behaviour, and it is the code, rather than God himself, which is worshipped. But moral dogmatism is not confined to religion, nor even to reactionary moralists of any kind. So-called permissiveness, in a peculiar way, breeds its own mores which can be equally restrictive on genuine freedom and responsibility, and which require acceptance if one is to belong to the group in which they are the norm. In some quarters, *not* to fiddle the expense accounts as a normal thing, *not* to look for a sleeping-partner at every party, becomes an offence.

Faith, however, is freedom in relation to God. His grace and our trust make this relationship. Again, we turn to Paul who fought for this freedom. Against those who would try to impose a legalistic conformity on membership of the Christian community as the way to salvation – adherence to the rite of circumcision, for example – he argues:

> For freedom Christ has set us free; stand fast, therefore, and do not submit again to a yoke of slavery. Now I, Paul, say to you that if you receive circumcision, Christ will be of no advantage to you. I testify again to every man who receives circumcision that he is bound to keep the whole law. You are severed from Christ, you who would be justified by the law; you have fallen away from grace. For through the Spirit, by faith, we await the hope of righteousness. For in Christ Jesus neither circumcision nor uncircumcision is of any avail, but faith working through love (Gal. 5.1–6).

No external code may interpose itself between ourselves and God.

God himself broke through such systems in Jesus who died as an accursed criminal, identifying himself with the moral and spiritual failures that we are, that we might share his son-like relationship to God. We are free therefore from the law as an external, arbitrary power over against us. And now we are free to do what the law actually points towards, namely, righteous living. Only, such conduct is not now an artificial code imposed on us from outside. It is the natural direction for those who are sons of God. For the 'law' of God is summed up in love. We are free – to be 'servants of one another' through love (Gal. 5.13), 'for the whole law is fulfilled in one word, "You shall love your neighbour as yourself"' (5.14). The moral code is still necessary for the obedience of fools and the guidance of wise men. We need help in deciding what is loving and just. But now it is the instrument of our new personal freedom with God, not an inhuman regulator of our lives. 'The Sabbath was made for man, not man for the Sabbath' (Mark 2.27).

Fourth, the freedom of faith is *freedom from authoritarianism and freedom for participation in community*. By obedient trust in the gracious God I am related to him as child to the Father. Just as there is no impersonal barrier of law between me and God, so there is no human person in the way either. If I must speak of some intermediary, it is Jesus Christ alone, for my relationship to God is a participation in Christ's own relationship of faith and obedience. My status and standing as a person is of one who, in face of God, has no rights or claims, yet who has been marvellously called, accepted and affirmed as of utter worth to God by his forgiving grace. I am freed from the urge to make false and pretentious claims for myself, and from the false, supine humility which too readily accepts domination by others. To exalt myself is to deny that I live only through God's *grace*. To abase myself is, equally, to deny that I am in fact *given* that grace.

Faith, then, means that there will be no lording it over others, nor abject submission to others. Others are not set over us absolutely, nor under us absolutely, but all are called equally to be participants in God's grace. This is the basis of *community*. It does not mean that faith sees no need for a certain structure of authority whether in the church, the family, the state, or any human institution. But no authority apart from God himself is ultimate. Human authorities are valid in so far as they themselves conform to the will and purpose of God.

Be subject for the Lord's sake to every human institution, whether it be to the emperor as supreme, or to governors as sent by him to punish those who do wrong and to praise those who do right. For it is God's will that by doing right you should put to silence the ignorance of foolish men. Live as free men, yet without using your freedom as a pretext for evil; but live as servants of God. Honour all men. Love the brotherhood. Fear God. Honour the emperor (I Peter 2.13–17).

Note that in this passage the authorities do not have any absolute power and authority *per se*. They possess authority in their function of maintaining a just and moral order in the world. Once the authority and the moral order diverge, it becomes the case that 'We must obey God rather than men' (Acts 5.29).

It must be candidly admitted that in practice the freedom of faith has all too often been crushed beneath the weight of authoritarianism, both in the church and in society. As far as the church is concerned, the Inquisition is but the most extreme manifestation of a tendency to turn the pastoral care *of* the faithful into an arrogant rule *over* them. The church's true authority lies in its pointing towards the one true and absolute authority of God himself. When the church or its leaders arrogate that authority to themselves, and claim that in themselves they can impose it in virtue of their position, they have interposed themselves between faith and God. Freedom and the gospel are forfeited. This has happened not only in the worst excesses of the Roman Catholic Church, but in many varieties of Protestantism which have become in their own way as authoritarian as the tradition they rejected.

It must equally be admitted that at times the role of religion in society has been to serve the interests of the oppressor. To comfort the oppressed with the thought that in heaven all will be equal is an old-established way of making more bearable the miseries and injustices of the present. But the freedom of faith can be the ferment in society at least as much as the opium of the people. The owners of the plantations in the West Indies quite rightly saw a long-term threat to their interests posed by the activities of the early missionaries among the slaves. The freedom of faith can be manifested in a rejection of the dehumanizing status thrust upon oneself. 'By faith in Christ I know I am a

child of God. I was a nobody – but now I'm a somebody' – so I
have heard a young man giving his testimony in one of the black
churches in this country. He was affirming his freedom in face of
a society which rejects him. There *is* an egalitarian thrust generated
by a gospel which brings people into an equally free and direct
access to God. It creates a vision of community in which people
recognize that, dependent on God and loved by God as they all
are, all do belong together. As Hans Küng says: 'The Church
itself should be a place of *equality of rights* and an *advocate of
equality of rights in the world*.'[2]

Fifth, the freedom of faith is *freedom from captivity to the world and
freedom for mastery over the world*. As was pointed out in chapter 2,
as conscious human persons we are aware of a distinctness between ourselves and the reality around us, and at the same time
we have to relate ourselves to that reality in a responsible and
creative way. All too often, however, we do not take full responsibility for ourselves in face of what is 'other' to us. We allow that
'other' to dominate us and control us, subverting our growth as
fully personal beings. To take an extremely dramatic case, in time
of war or grave threat of war, the citizens of a country can be
caught up in a wave of nationalistic and patriotic hysteria which
obliterates any rational and realistic assessment of the situation,
which sees the enemy as a total blackguard and one's own nation
as an angel of light. Less dramatically, but no less potentially
dangerous, is the way in which racist attitudes can be unthinkingly assumed towards ethnic groups within society, and people
stigmatized as inferior or threatening regardless of their actual
behaviour. Or there is the power of the nebulous but very real
ethos of a society to condition our aims and values: the assumption, for instance, that the greatest happiness of the greatest
number will best be ensured by the pursuit of individual prosperity. We are fatefully prone to let ourselves be carried along by
the attitudes of the mass. Nor is this power of what is 'other'
purely psychological. The organizations we build to develop and
use our resources reveal an inbuilt tendency to develop a life of
their own without regard to actual human needs. The business
which began by smelting ore on a small scale develops into a
transnational corporation with more effective power than many
of the countries in which it operates, and is accountable to none of
them. The trade union which was founded, and still exists, to

protect the interests of workers grows into a body which at times seems to wield its power in a way that serves the interests of no one, whether belonging to it or not. The welfare state, created to eliminate human degradation and poverty, produces its own bureaucracies of files and forms and inaccessible officials. In face of such collectivities, we often feel helpless and simply prepared to let our lives be run by 'them'. Power, and structures of power, must be recognized as essential. But all too often it appears that it is man who is made for the structures, instead of the reverse.

In the world of the first century, Paul spoke of 'elemental spirits of the universe' (Gal. 4.3, 9; Col. 2.8) which 'enslave' men; of 'principalities and powers' (Rom. 8.38; Eph. 3.10; 6.12, Col. 1.16); of 'angels' (Col. 2.18). Such beings and powers were regarded as superhuman forces in the world, often related to heavenly bodies (and note the continued and possibly increasing modern belief in astrology) which determine men's lives, requiring appeasement by religious and ascetic rituals. In the Graeco-Roman world, such quasi-divine powers were regarded as real entities, powers to be feared and placated. Paul himself may well have regarded their existence as real. But, crucially, he saw them as put in their proper place by Christ. God 'disarmed the principalities and powers and made a public example of them, triumphing over them in [Christ]' (Col. 2.15). Not in any of these powers, but only in God himself, lies real security for humans. Not to any of these powers, but only to God himself, do men owe absolute loyalty and obedience. Jesus lived a life of total freedom from them by his utter trust and obedience consummated in the cross, and his resurrection is the signal of his triumph over them. Those who through Jesus put their obedient trust in God are triumphantly free with him over all these false claimants to human worship, trust and service.

In other words, faith, by bringing us into direct access to God, breaks the power which all that is *not God* may have over us. The false allurements and threats by which we were bound to the world are subdued. But the world is still there. We cannot live detached from it, nor escape from it. For it is still the world which God has created and loves, and in which he wills his purpose to be realized. Freed from false captivity to the world and its powers, we are able to turn to it again to fight and overcome the powers, and to use the world for its proper ends. So faith becomes the fulcrum of responsibility in fighting all that makes man less than human, the collective misuses of power which rob man of his dignity, the technological greed that despoils the earth, the fears that breed racism and a nuclear arms race, and the insidious creeping apathy which increasingly privatizes critizens' interests in the face of public evils.

Thus faith, by being brought into living relationship with God, realizes that the world is not godlike, nor does any power within it have divine status over us. Idolatry is recognized for what it is. The world is 'de-divinized' in face of the only true God. The world is not thereby devalued, but is restored to its true status as God's creation. And man, as the Bible profoundly teaches, is called to be God's agent or steward in caring for the world and enabling it to be what God wants it to be. Man is to 'have dominion' over it (Gen. 2.28). God has 'made him little less than God' and has 'put all things under his feet' (Ps. 8.5, 6). Jesus, 'crowned with glory and honour' is the pioneer in actually realizing this glorious human destiny (Heb. 2.9) and therefore those who are related to God through him already have some experience of the freedom over the world which he has won. This is more than a speculative idea. There is, to say the least, a good deal of circumstantial evidence that the biblical belief in creation played a decisive part in the rise of the modern scientific outlook in the West.[3] Such a belief inculcates a view of the world as nondivine but real, as reliable and orderly because it is the creation of a faithful and orderly Creator, and therefore as amenable to rational investigation and use.

Faith, therefore is a freedom: a freedom overcoming the captivities of personal self-centredness, legalism, moralism, and authoritarianism, a freedom releasing us from bondage to the past and the would-be powers of the world. Humanly speaking, it appears to be a very frail freedom when set against the massive weight of the powers ranged against it within ourselves, our institutions and the world at large. It is like a young plant, a root out of dry ground – which can yet crack and split the concrete slab laid over it. For the strength of faith does not spring from the man who has it, but from God who gives it.

9

Faith as Understanding

Throughout this book, we have looked at faith as a direct, personal relationship of trust in God: a living, or existential, relationship of the believer to the One whom he or she obediently trusts. What has been stressed is *belief in* God, rather than *belief about* God, that is, faith as an intellectual acceptance of ideas concerning God – his existence, nature, activity and so forth – and the various items of 'Christian belief'. This stress has been deliberate, to emphasize the fact that the faith by which one lives the Christian life is this faith as personal trust in the God who meets us with his grace. It is so apt to be lost amid the concern for other things about which, like Martha, we are so busy.

But while faith as personal trust in God is central, faith as 'belief that' cannot be ignored. There *is* an intellectual aspect to faith, and to fail to take it with proper seriousness is as much a distortion as to make it the only element of importance. What matters is to keep the intellectual side in perspective. We cannot grasp the living God by a purely intellectual exercise, for faith is a movement of our whole selves in trust. But precisely because our whole selves are involved, the intellectual element comes into play. The intellect, our capacity to understand, to grasp meaning, is a real part of us regardless of whether we consider ourselves to be 'intellectuals' or not. There is a fashionable modern tendency to decry the intellect. 'Too cerebral' is a vogue criticism. Yet one cannot grasp what 'too cerebral' means without some cerebral effort. The movements promoting personal growth and sensitivity are highly desirable and welcome, recognizing as they do that to be a human person involves bodily and emotional life, and that these elements play a bigger part in our existence than we normally imagine. But to attempt to deny the place of the thinking mind is as much an evasion as to run away from the fact of our sub-conscious drives.

We do not exist solely by thinking and reflection, but we cannot exist without them. As human persons, it has been stressed in earlier chapters, our lives mature in relationship with others. The mark of our humanity is the capacity to *meet* another, to enter into a relationship with the other as a *Thou* (to use Martin Buber's terminology), as distinct from looking upon the other in a detached way as an *It*. But, as Buber himself was careful to say, we cannot live solely in the realm of *Thou*.[1] Any glance at our personal relationships will bear this out. The most intense form of I-Thou relationship, that of love between man and woman, generates the need for detached reflection no less than its being at heart a mutual giving and receiving. Lovers gaze into each others' eyes, lost in each other. But if their relationship is to deepen and blossom into a stable partnership, it requires the lovers, together and individually, to step back mentally from their embraces and think *about* themselves and each other, the possibilities and the pitfalls, the hopes and the realities, of what a continuing commitment would mean. A responsible relationship includes reflection no less than involvement, for the sake of the relationship itself.

To understand is to grasp the coherence, the connectedness of something. To indulge for a moment in a bit of naive literalism, understanding is a matter of 'standing under'. Suppose for the first time in your life you are being driven across a bridge like, for instance, Brunel's Clifton Suspension Bridge, and your companion says 'What a marvellous construction this is!' You may not fully grasp what he means. But you will, if he takes you down on to the road that runs along the bottom of the gorge so that you can literally stand under it, and see the whole symmetry of piles, cables and girders and their connections with the natural rock faces. By stepping away from it and under it, you are now able to see it as a whole, and the way in which it relates to the surrounding landscape, in a way that you could not have done when on the bridge itself. So too, we only fully understand a novel or story when we have read the whole; and the 'meaning' of individual events comes out fully only when we know the whole, and see their part in that whole.

Understanding in this way is the prerequisite of life, which would otherwise be a chaotic jumble of experiences. We need continuity, coherence, purpose. We need pictures, frames of reference, mental maps of what constitutes our world, so that we may know what our own part in it is. When we encounter the unexpected and puzzling, we try to deal with it by relating it what we understand already. When the young child wakes crying in the small hours, clearly unwell but unable to explain just how, the parents respond by trying to identify the trouble in terms of their picture of likely children's ailments, built out of past experience and maybe Dr Spock. A cold? Tummy upset? Incipient measles? They look for likely explanations in terms of this framework of understanding. They may need to call in the doctor, because the trouble proves to be beyond their capacity to identify and deal with, in which case their understanding will be enlarged by his. But at certain points in the human quest for understanding, a new discovery may prove impossible to relate to the accepted framework of reference as it stands. It bursts through the picture of wholeness and coherence which has become accepted, and demands that a wholly new one be constructed. When Madame Curie noticed that in the presence of radium, covered photographic plates clouded over, a fact emerged which could not be accounted for in terms of the physical view of the universe dating from Newton onwards, and it signalled the dawn of the new era of atomic physics.

Nor can faith, for its part, avoid the quest for an understanding of the reality with which it deals. If it has not been raised already, then certainly with faith there is raised the question of the most fundamental understanding of what the universe is which we inhabit, and of what is most fully real. Is the contingent world in which we live and of which we are part, the world of nature and the world of human history, alone real, by itself? Is that all there is? Or is it grounded in a transcendent, ultimate reality to which it owes its existence? At least implicitly, faith works with the latter picture of understanding. To believe *in* God clearly carries within it the *belief that* God is real. 'For whoever would draw near to God must believe that he exists and that he rewards those who seek him' (Heb. 11.6). Two extremes must be avoided here. One is the view that a personal faith in God, as has been explored in most of this book, can be built solely out of this ultimate understanding. The other is that such faith in God is quite independent of such fundamental views of the universe and ultimate reality, being a purely existential orientation of oneself. If one believes in God, even if it is the case that one cannot produce a compelling intellectual proof of God's reality to satisfy the disinterested enquirer, one is at least implicitly asserting that God's reality is a reasonable possibility to be maintained. On the one hand, if one approaches God starting along the route of intellectual understanding, there comes a point where the decision, the leap, of faith is required. In the first place, to choose the understanding of the universe as grounded in a transcendent, ultimate reality as against the view of the universe as purely self-subsistent, is a matter of fundamental decision of an intuitive kind. In the second place, to perceive that ultimate reality as gracious and to entrust oneself to it is to enter into faith in the fullest sense. On the other hand, one's entry into a living faith may not have been accompanied by such explicit and conscious intellectual steps. But if that faith is more than a wilful decision to behave in a certain way, if it is a claim to be in relationship to what is not of this world, yet real, then it demands some effort at understanding. Just what is the relationship of this strange reality called God, to the rest of our experience? It is an exaggeration to say, with Martin Buber, that one does not need to know anything *about* God in order to believe in him.

Nor can we regard faith as a matter of sheer 'experience', compared with which all reflective reasoning about faith is a mere coating of words. This is to make an impossible divorce between reality and language, between experience and the words we use to describe and interpret experience. There can be no absolutely wordless apprehension of 'experience'. Words are the means by which experiences are mediated to us for understanding, even if at times the words seem barely adequate to convey the reality. As Peter Donovan puts it, to look for a 'pure experience' without any interpretation of it is rather like looking for a 'pure hole' with no surroundings to it.[2]

In saying, then, that in faith we relate to God in trust, we must admit that here as elsewhere we are involved in language, understanding and interpretation. There must be reflection as well as involvement. We have to 'stand under' the relationship as well as stand in it. Precisely because we have been brought so intimately into relation with God, there is a new, ultimate wholeness to our life to be grasped. The meaning of our life in relation to God, and the meaning of God in relation to our life, has to be sought. The meaning of faith for all the other relationships in our existence awaits exploration. Otherwise faith remains an odd, quirkish extra to our life, instead of its basis and direction. Faith demands to become the most inclusive frame of reference for our lives, our most embracing picture of ourselves and our world in the ultimate environment of God.

The need for understanding in faith is grounded not simply in these general considerations, however. As was seen in chapter 4, specifically Christian faith arises as response to a message. Christian faith is not communicated as a wordless, mystical cloud of feeling or purely inner revelation in the soul. It is communicated through a message, a story, the particular story of Jesus, which moreover on the lips of the witness is already an interpreted story. It is the story of Jesus as the way, the truth and the life, which is told. Further, as we have seen, faith is confessed in acts which include verbal affirmations. 'Jesus is Lord', the earliest and simplest Christian confession, expressive of the basic personal trust and obedience of the believer, may not appear a very 'intellectual' statement. But it is a considered act of understanding, for it is making a decisive connection between two ideas: that of Jesus, who was crucified, and that of Lord, the one who is triumphant by God's power and worthy of allegiance above all others.

From that point on, Christian faith could not avoid the development of an *understanding* of the faith. For even such a simple expression as 'Jesus is Lord' is charged with innumerable questions and possible implications. If Jesus was to be called Lord what, for example, did this mean for the attitude of Christians towards the state and the cult of emperor-worship? More profoundly, if Jesus was 'Lord', what did this imply for his relationship to the One called 'Lord' in the Old Testament, God himself? Christian faith as message and confession thus carried within itself from the start the necessity of reflection and understanding, the more so as the Christian movement spread beyond the boundaries of Judaism in which it was born, into the Graeco–Roman world with its very different cultural thought-forms and ways of understanding God and the world.

In other words, theology is necessary. One cannot relate to God without at least some thinking about this relationship, about the God to whom one relates, and the implications of faith for one's whole life as a person in the world. There is no Christian without a theology of some sort. Of course theology in the more customary technical sense of a disciplined and systematic study of the subject-matter of faith in its more refined reaches, is the concern of relatively few. But between, say, the discussion taking place in a baptismal or confirmation class of young teenagers, and a university seminar on the Council of Chalcedon, there is no absolute gulf. There are varying degrees of conceptualization and depth of study of the Christian tradition, but no hard and fast divisions. Ministers particularly, who try to show that they are really down-to-earth, practical types by saying 'I'm no theologian . . .' should know better. It is precisely because the life of the Christian and the church is such a practical business, that theology is necessary. Effective and purposeful action in any sphere requires that we know what we should be doing, and why. Christian action, if it is not to degenerate into a trivial and irrelevant busyness, requires continued assessment against faith's picture of what is ultimately true, needful, and important in a world which belongs to God. That is what theology is about.

The suspicion of 'theologizing' is justified in so far as the mind is prone to detach thinking from actual living, and to pursue thought for its own sake. Faith, we have seen, inevitably produces theology, for we are understanding beings and the gospel is a message which implies a particular understanding in its call for trust and commitment. But theology can become detached from faith. The effort to understand can take on a life of its own, and its basis in faith can be forgotten. The whole of reality, even God himself, can be assumed to be comprehensible by intellectual effort, and faith comes to be regarded as a makeshift affair suitable only for those not clever enough to grasp truth by reasoning. It has been a constant peril in Western Christian thought so to intellectualize the apprehension of God that the basic element of personal trust is forgotten. Faith then comes to be seen as something that *follows* understanding as an optional extra, or as a stage on the way to understanding which then leaves mere faith behind.

Had Western thought listened more carefully to St Augustine, who gave the West much of its intellectual apparatus for a thousand years and more, the mistake would have been made less often. Augustine wrote: 'Understanding is the reward of faith. Therefore do not seek to understand in order to believe, but believe in order that you may understand (*crede ut intelligas*); for unless you believe, you will not understand.'[3] One who did listen to Augustine, seven centuries later, was Anselm of Canterbury, who built Augustine's insight into his own view of theology as *fides quaerens intellectum*: faith seeking understanding. We must try to understand what we believe, not so that having reached understanding we may do away with faith, but so that faith may be the more cogent, and the teaching of the church more coherent and effective.

As we have seen, Martin Luther made personal, trusting faith in the gracious God the keystone of his theology. In the generations that followed the Reformation, however, Protestant theologians formulated a view of faith comprising three elements: *notitia* (knowledge), *assensus* (assent) and *fiducia* (trust). This certainly attempted to comprehend the wholeness of faith, but it ran the risk of schematizing faith in an artificial way. It gives the impression that the route to faith is, first, the acquisition of knowledge of what is to be believed, in the sense of doctrinal propositions about God, Christ and so forth. Then, one becomes intellectually convinced of the truth of these statements. Finally, one makes an act of trust and personal commitment to the truth of these statements. It is very doubtful whether the customary practice of faith follows this scheme. It is probably more often the case that a person finds himself or herself becoming existentially involved with the claims and offer of Jesus, leading to a new-found trust in God, and from that situation of *fiducia* moves in the direction of *assensus* and *notitia*. But it would be better still not to try to separate the three elements out in this way as though they were independent items. It is the basic feature of faith as an actual relationship to God which is ignored by this formula, with its assumptions that it is primarily statements about God, rather than God himself, in which faith rests. Not, as we have insisted, that we can believe in God without using statements about him, but that it is perilously easy to look to these statements without actual encounter with the One to whom they refer. As Ronald Gregor Smith wrote:

So the power of faith cannot be reduced to the authoritative demand that you accept a series of pronouncements whose guarantee is in the last resort a man-made guarantee, whether it is the authority of Pope, or bible, creed or council. For the true power of faith resides in the gracious act of God in Christ, offering a new start to human existence. The basic objection, therefore, to the traditional threefold formula, with all its variations, is not that it misses the mark entirely, and not that it so easily tips over into an exaggeration of one or another of its elements, but that it tends to petrify in inadequate categories an essentially dynamic situation. It is not able to cope with the offence of the gracious act of God in Christ.[4]

Gregor Smith is here pointing up a tension which cannot be avoided in the Christian tradition. Faith naturally and inevitably seeks understanding, producing statements varying from the elemental and spontaneous expressions of faith and devotion, to highly refined conceptual arguments and formulae, and moreover certain credal and doctrinal statements regarded as crucially *authoritative* for faith. Notably, the statements produced by the great councils of Nicaea and Chalcedon in the fourth and fifth centuries respectively are regarded as the classic, authoritative statements regarding the relationship of Christ to God the Father, and the nature of the person of Christ as fully divine and fully human in one. Once we allow that faith seeks understanding, the possibility of false understanding has to be recognized, and to be distinguished from correct, or orthodox, belief. Today, the situation is complicated by the fact that the 'authoritative' statements of the early church are couched in language and thought-forms of an age quite different from our own. Any sharp, clear-cut claims to absolute authority are weathered and blurred by history. But the real tension is not so much the tension between the concepts of the early centuries and the outlook of today, but between all conceptualization which is in the end a *human* affair – even when enshrined in ecclesiastical authority – and the living God himself. As we have insisted, faith does not apprehend or experience God without language and interpretation. But to assent to verbalized formulae does not in itself guarantee that one is entering into what Gregor Smith calls the 'essentially dynamic situation' of the relationship with God.

Faith cannot do without the tradition of understanding. Even the basic message of Jesus as God's grace derives from the tradition. It is available in the present only because it has been handed on. The believer, in appropriating the living, personal relationship with God, is simply entering into an inheritance bequeathed by all the saints. And the tradition of understanding is to be seen as the way in which, in succeeding ages, the church has sought to preserve that free and direct access to God in Christ. The doctrines and creeds fail in their purpose if they come to be regarded as intellectualized substitutes for that apprehension of faith, the unity in relationship to God. They are large-scale maps giving overall landmarks for those wishing to plot their personal approach to God. To read the accounts of the fierce christological controversies in the early centuries is admittedly rather like visiting an ancient battlefield where a few burial mounds remain, but none of the passion which spilt the blood. But what was at stake in those debates was more than the satisfaction of the theological intellect for its own sake. Behind the refutation of the Arian view that the Son was of 'like' substance with the Father as distinct from the 'same' substance, more than a Greek diphthong was at issue. It was, at heart, the issue of whether or not in Jesus Christ man really is brought into direct communion with God. It was not a neat theological formula, but a Christ who can really save, really bring sinful men to God, whom the Fathers wished to assert. With such a Christ, it was the directness and the freedom of faith which was equally, if less overtly, at stake. It was because such a faith in God through Christ was at work, that the debate sprang from such roots of passion.

In its search for understanding, therefore, faith continues to live in its own reality in the present, as a free and immediate relationship of trust in God through Christ. But it will know that it can only remain itself, and can only develop its understanding, as it pays regard to the tradition. In themselves, the classic doctrines and creeds are not absolute, authoritatively binding formulae, for that would hinder faith's immediacy of access to God. It would be putting a form of understanding before faith. But they are the classic signposts for faith's understanding, pointers towards the reality which is apprehended in trust. To quote Gregor Smith again:

Faith demands to be understood. And as soon as this demand is honestly faced, the traditional doctrines play their part: not as normative, not as a substitute for faith, but as servants in the house of faith. Faith without doctrine is a wildly swaying weathercock, driven around by every gust of the arbitrary imagination or speculative power of men. Doctrine without faith is a sullen and joyless taskmaster, the slavedriver with the whip. There is no immutable doctrine; but the reality of the doctrinal tradition keeps faith from fantasy. The two must go together; but the greater of the two is faith.[5]

Faith's search for understanding will never be concluded, whether in the life of an individual believer or in the course of the household of faith, the church, through history. Indeed, the classic doctrinal statements of the early church, while warning of certain understandings as false views of Christ, did not thereby claim that their own formulations were complete, exact and final definitions of the truth. They rather outlined certain areas of mystery which, if not yet capable of precise and fully satisfying explanation, were not to be short-circuited by a too-hasty desire to 'understand'. They did not conclude debates and questions, but generated new ones. St Augustine, who investigated the belief in the triune nature of God more exhaustively than any theologian before him (and, possibly, since) confessed that he wrote of such things in order that he might not be completely silent. Faith, knowing that it is brought into encounter with the living God, is filled with a passion to understand what this means, and at the same time knows that inherent in its situation is something which will always elude final understanding. Just because faith knows God to be absolutely *other* than us yet absolutely *for* us in his grace, there is both understanding and confession of not-understanding. To be brought into relationship to God does not mean that thereby we shall know all about him. Our experience of relationship with other people will teach us that, precisely as we are brought into closer and more intimate contact with a person, the more we are struck by the unfathomable otherness and uniqueness of that person. The closer we come to a person and 'know' him, the more we are aware of the mystery of that person's being. The other person transcends us, and the more we know of that other person, the more acutely aware we become of that transcendence. Personal relationships can go astray when we take the other person for granted. We have a neat, stereotyped picture of the other person which we assume is all that needs to be said of him – we can 'read him like a book'. Sooner or later, we find the real person smashing through that image. And if ever we think we have pinned *God* down in a final formula or doctrine, or finally explained how Jesus is both God's fullest being for man and man's being for God, we can be certain that it is not God but an idol that we are dealing with. Michael Polanyi writes of the way in which the Christian thinker 'indwells' an idea or theory arising from his faith:

> The indwelling of the Christian worshipper is therefore a continual attempt at breaking out, at casting off the condition of man, even while humbly acknowledging the inescapability. Such indwelling is fulfilled most completely when it increases this effort to the utmost. It resembles not the dwelling within a great theory of which we enjoy the complete understanding, nor an immersion in the pattern of a musical masterpiece, but the heuristic upsurge which strives to break through the accepted formulations of thought, guided by the intimations of discoveries still beyond our horizon. Christian worship sustains, as it were, an eternal, never to be consummated hunch: a heuristic vision which is accepted for the sake of its unresolvable tension. It is like an obsession with a problem known to be insoluble, which yet follows, against reason, unswervingly, the heuristic command: 'Look at the unknown!' Christianity sedulously fosters, and in a sense permanently satisfies, man's craving for mental dissatisfaction by offering him the comfort of a crucified God.[6]

An eternal, never to be consummated hunch: that is an admirable restatement, from a modern philosopher, of Anselm's 'faith seeking understanding'. But it should not be thought that this search for understanding is directed solely towards God himself, or Christ, or any of the other 'mysteries of religion', in isolation. The believer does not face God in a vacuum, but in the context of life and all its relationships in the world. Faith is not just concerned with God, but seeks an understanding of the world in the light of the God known to faith. The God in whom faith rests is the Creator – of all things visible and invisible. There is then nothing, quite literally nothing, in human experience which is not raw material to be worked on by faith seeking understanding. As was pointed out in the previous chapter, there is evidence that it was an understanding of the world as *creation* which played a vital part in the rise of the modern natural sciences. Theology is not just the science of God. It is not just reflection about God. It is reflection upon life and its experiences in the light of faith in God. This in fact for 'lay' Christians is what theology must primarily mean. The so-called secular realm is no mere adjunct to faith's interest, nor even the stage-setting for its activity. For it is through the issues thrust up by human affairs, issues which pose questions about the values, purpose and significance of human life, that faith is stirred into new movements of understanding. If life is at bottom grounded in God's creative purpose and activity, if it is man in his humanity to whom God seeks to offer himself in his graciousness, then a theological issue lies latent within each and every question about how life is to be ordered, whether in the role of the family today, or in industrial relations, or the uses of nuclear technology, or the place of leisure in modern society, or the treatment of offenders . . . or whatever. This is not to be confused with the banal idea that to every problem there must be a 'Christian' answer. The believer has no monopoly of truth, and his faith in God does not make him a specially privileged guru. He has as much to learn as anyone else, and may often need to learn it from those who do not share his faith. It is simply that his faith can lend insights and raise questions because of its perspective of life disclosed in Christ, the decisive clue to the purpose and fulfilment of being human. At times the contribution of faith will be less a matter of making a particular statement, than the injection of a certain attitude. Faith knows of the profound depths of sinfulness, the insidious tendency of the human self to mistake itself as the source and centre of wisdom and security. Faith will therefore be a check on utopian idealism. But equally, faith knows the astonishing fact of God's grace. The cross is the counter to both superficial optimism and black despair, being the revelation alike of the potentialities of evil and the redemptive victory of love. Faith understands that there is hope in a seemingly intractable problem, even when the hope cannot yet be clearly seen and defined.

10

Faith as Exploration

This book has tried to do some justice to the wholeness of faith. The reader is going to be disappointed, however, if it is expected that this final chapter will provide a neat summing up and conclusion of the way that has been taken, as though the wholeness of faith had been circumscribed and could now, give or take the odd loose end in need of tying up, be deposited in a bag for safe keeping. Faith is not so manageable. For, as has been seen from the start, faith is marked by a looking away to the reality in which it trusts. It is an openness to what is other, and this openness always makes faith a somewhat provisional, restless and dissatisfied business in its own eyes. At the end of the first chapter, mention was made of Karl Barth's warning that it is a bad thing when Christianity pays too much attention to faith, at the expense of the God in whom faith is placed. Faith, by its very own nature, must not be too interested in itself, not even in drawing its thinking about itself to an impressive finale. It has other things to be getting on with, as in the parable:

Will any one of you, who has a servant plowing or keeping sheep, say to him when he has come in from the field, 'Come at once and sit down at table?' Will he not rather say to him, 'Prepare supper for me, and gird yourself and serve us, till I eat and drink; and afterward you shall eat and drink'? Does he thank the servant because he did what was commanded? So you also, when you have done all that is commanded you, say, 'We are unworthy servants; we have only done what was our duty' (Luke 17.7–9).

Faith, it has been seen, is trust in the reliability of something or someone other than ourselves, and Christian faith is trust in the gracious God known in Jesus. Faith decides to trust, but it is not its decision that it makes so much of, rather the One who calls for that decision and enables it to be made. Faith confesses itself outwardly, not in order to advertise itself, but so that the whole person may concretely enter into faith. Faith obeys and serves in a commitment not to itself but to God and to others. It enjoys a freedom, but not a freedom which is an independent possession of the believer to relish on his or her own, rather a freedom in relationship to God and to others. Faith seeks understanding, but never reaches a complete and rounded understanding, for it is attached to a reality beyond final comprehension. We 'walk by faith, not by sight' (II Cor. 5.7). Faith looks beyond itself from start to finish, and a book on faith can be neither unduly long nor over dogmatic in its conclusions.

Faith includes a kind of self-forgetfulness, for it is continually in search of what lies ahead and beyond. Paul, having stated so eloquently the reality of union with Christ by faith, goes on:

> Not that I have already obtained this or am already perfect; but I press on to make it my own, because Christ Jesus has made me his own. Brethren, I do not consider that I have made it my own; but one thing I do, forgetting what lies behind and straining forward to what lies ahead, I press on toward the goal for the prize of the upward call of God in Christ Jesus (Phil. 3.12–14).

Similarly the writer to the Hebrews, whom we noted in chapter 2 as supplying the only formal definition of faith in the New Testament, illustrates the 'assurance of things hoped for, the conviction of things not seen' with a procession of witnesses who were able to act adventurously and courageously because they glimpsed greater possibilities beyond their immediate situation. Abraham went out 'not knowing where he was to go', but holding to the promise that somewhere, sometime, God had prepared a 'better country' for him and his family. Moses looked beyond the oppression and corruption of Egypt 'to the reward', knowing that through endurance of suffering and abuse would come eventual liberation. And so through all the heroes of faith, who triumphed through suffering, in hope of God's completed purpose. Christians,

likewise, are to persevere and look forward, their eyes on
Jesus 'the pioneer and perfecter of our faith' who himself was the
great exemplar of hope and trust in enduring the cross for the
sake of the joy that lay beyond.

Faith lives and grows while it does not take itself seriously. It
takes *Christ* seriously, with all the risk and cost that this involves
in human terms. In so forgetting itself, it finds itself. In so risking
itself, it is preserved. In dying, it lives. It is thankful for what it
has hitherto experienced and apprehended of God, but it does not
regard yesterday's experience as the exact norm for today, nor
today's as the certain norm for tomorrow. It believes in Jesus
Christ as the same yesterday, today and forever – the same in his
trustworthiness as God's self-disclosure and our true humanity –
but does not expect there to be any single absolute, permanent
expression of commitment to him, or understanding of him in
doctrinal terms.

This self-forgetfulness of faith counteracts the tendency to
visualize what the ideal Christian looks like, and to attempt to
wear that ideal, which so often disguises a hidden self-admiration.
Those captivated by Jesus have no time and no need to be pre-
occupied with themselves in this way. They know they are safe
enough with him, and share with him in the delights and the
sufferings of the world around them. Faith is not the cultivation of
an ideal for ourselves, but the abandoning of ourselves, through
Christ, to God in the power of the Spirit. 'If any man would come
after me, let him deny himself and take up his cross and follow me.
For whoever would save his life will lose it; and whoever loses his
life for my sake and the gospel's will save it' (Mark 8.34f.). Even
this stark challenge of Jesus can be perverted by our desire for self-
idealization, and used for our personal aggrandisement. How
great to be thought of as sharing the cross of Christ! How we
would love the halo of martyrdom! What a glow we can feel when
we think we are suffering for a righteous cause! We have over-
looked what in fact Jesus says. We have grasped our cross before
denying ourselves, and we have put ourselves on the cross, that
we might so conspicuously be seen to be heroes. We cannot pick
up the cross if our hands are still full of ourselves. Dietrich
Bonhoeffer's famous words, written when the likelihood of his
own martyrdom had suddenly become intensely real with the
failure of the plot on Hitler's life, cannot be quoted too often:

... I'm still discovering right up to this moment, that it is only by living completely in this world that one learns to have faith. One must completely abandon any attempt to make something of oneself, whether it be a saint, or a converted sinner, or a churchman (a so-called priestly type!), a righteous man or an unrighteous one, a sick man or a healthy one. By this-worldliness I mean living unreservedly in life's duties, problems, successes and failures, experiences and perplexities. In so doing we throw ourselves into the arms of God, taking seriously, not our own sufferings, but those of God in the world – watching with Christ in Gethsemane. That, I think, is faith; that is *metanoia*; and that is how one becomes a man and a Christian (cf. Jer. 45!). How can success make us arrogant, or failure lead us astray, when we share in God's sufferings through a life of this kind?[1]

Relatively few readers of Bonhoeffer, perhaps, have bothered to look up his reference to Jeremiah 45. The word of the prophet to his faithful secretary Baruch, when the end was coming upon Jerusalem, is a cutting away of all self-made hopes, and a pointer to the only real hope, which is that God will give what he intends to give, and that will be enough:

Thus says the Lord, the God of Israel, to you, O Baruch: You said, 'Woe is me! for the Lord has added sorrow to my pain; I am weary with my groaning, and I find no rest'. Thus shall you say to him, Thus says the Lord: Behold, what I have built I am breaking down, and what I have planted I am plucking up – that is, the whole land. And do you seek great things for yourself? Seek them not; for, behold, I am bringing evil upon all flesh, says the Lord; but I will give you your life as a prize of war in all places to which you may go (Jer. 45.2–5).

Faith has a humble and joyful assurance that, as it meets whatever comes its way in the world, of responsibility or challenge, joy or suffering, success or failure, God is shaping the believer into becoming the person that he wills. That is, faith believes in providence, a providence which may be discerned in a much more profound way than is sometimes suggested by pious anecdotes of inexplicable deliverances (though it need not exclude them). The believer may be able to trace a thread of connections and direction in his or her life, not of his or her own making, recognized by faith as the hidden finger of the graciousness of the One who is ever seeking to give himself to us as disclosed in Christ, ever seeking to elicit from us the trust and commitment seen most fully in Christ, ever seeking to use us as his human agents to fulfil his purpose in the world, towards the end indicated by Christ. But the believer will be reticent in speaking about such things, for there are jagged rifts and impenetrable shadows in our personal stories, no less than in human history as a whole, which defy rationalization and even theologization for the time being. To repeat, faith is not sight, not even complete sight of ourselves. And however much we may think we can recognize the hand of grace in our story hitherto, the assurance that the same grace will be ours tomorrow is not quite like an extrapolation of the straight line of a graph beyond the points so far plotted on the paper. It is yet another act of trust, for another day.

But is not all this to skate round the *difference*, the discernible difference, that there should be between the Christian and the non-Christian? Shouldn't faith make a real change in a person's life, so that the believer 'stands out' among others? What about the righteousness of the disciples which should exceed even that of the scribes and pharisees? In view of all that has been said in this book, the believer certainly is different from others, through the discovery – the most profound discovery anyone can ever make – that his security lies not in himself but in God, and that the direction and fulfilment of his life are given in Christ. That is a peculiar vision given to faith. And if the believer lives by this vision, he will be different. But to ask to be different from others as the first requirement is to put the cart before the horse. 'And do you seek great things for yourself? Seek them not.' There is too much premature and frenetic anxiety among Christians on this point, too much asking how we can show ourselves more responsible than our run-of-the-mill neighbours, more compassionate than the humanists, more humane than the Marxists. We are called first and foremost to be true to what we see of Christ. We shall then be different enough, different as God wants us to be. We may well find ourselves becoming different in ways that we would not have chosen for ourselves.

For in the end, faith knows that God alone is truly good. Captivated by this goodness, faith will be forgetful and absent-minded about many other things. The Christian will continually be open to the reproach of not practising what he preaches. He himself will know agonizingly well the repeated and humiliating awareness of the gulf between his calling and his actual commitment. But he will not waste time and energy vociferously defending or justifying himself. He will know that often there is nothing that can be said in his defence, and once again he can only entrust himself to the forgiveness out of which can dawn a new day. He is less concerned to appear good in himself, than to be a witness to God's goodness. He will have a sense of humour, most of all about himself. Humour stems from incongruities, and what is more incongruous than grace for sinners?

The unceasing exploration of God's goodness and graciousness is faith's real business: new experiments of trust, new ventures of commitment, new areas of understanding. To be realistic, much of the impulse towards such exploration stems from the stern challenges and questions that faith has to face. We decide for faith, yet doubt is rarely absent, sometimes as a niggling question that can be left till another day, sometimes as a chilling midnight mockery that the whole business of faith is a childish stunt. Who would dare claim that his faith and his whole personality are completely integrated as yet? Who has yet sorted out satisfactorily the relationship of the discoveries of biological science to a Christian view of man? Or the relationship of Christianity to other faiths? A book such as this, even if it pleads its particular topic as a reason for its relative narrowness of scope, can only witness to the vulnerability of faith, humanly speaking, in face of the contemporary challenges to it. Above all, there are no fully satisfying solutions to the massive facts of evil and suffering in the world. We continually have to re-affirm our trust in the God revealed in Jesus, as in the end answering with his love the pain of the universe, even if at present we do not completely know *how* he does so. For faith, the balance is tipped less by a rational argument than a hunch that the foundation of all things is this love, not pain; grace, not death-ridden meaninglessness. If faith in God does not provide us with all the answers to the dark mysteries, it is just as sure that a finally dark universe does not square with what has been glimpsed and experienced in Christ, which stands in its own reality. 'Lord, to whom shall we go? You have the words of eternal life; and we have believed, and have come to know, that you are the Holy One of God' (John 6.68f.).

With the drawing of this Love and the voice of this Calling

We shall not cease from exploration
And the end of all our exploring
Will be to arrive where we started
And know the place for the first time.[2]

So the exploration goes on. We know God in Christ, yet realize how much more is to be apprehended. The exploration goes on through our listening to the scriptures and the whole tradition of witnesses of faith and understanding who have explored in the past. The exploration goes on through prayer, that waiting upon God in the Spirit till the point is reached when we find ourselves not simply looking to God, or thinking about him, nor just contemplating Christ; that point where we begin to notice that our thoughts are being moved by another than ourselves, in a direction other than our own, and we know we are with the Son crying 'Abba! Father!', being drawn further into his relationship of obedient trust. It continues as we discover more of ourselves, and we find that whatever we discover in ourselves, good or ill, can be yielded to God in trust for mercy, healing and renewal. The exploration turns with each crisis, each moment when the stability of our lives is shaken, when we see that 'things will never be the same again' but also find that a new and deeper security can be given from beyond ourselves, accompanied by a wider vision of what our life can be. It meets the ceaseless arrival of new questions in human society which call for new perspectives on the possibilities and responsibilities of human life. It embraces the suffering and the joy, God's travail and God's joy in the world. In a myriad ways, Christ as the consummation of God's graciousness to man and man's response to God, awaits the exploration of faith. Here and now, faith anticipates something of the meaning of eternal life, which is to 'know God' in all his manifestations, and thus means to be taken out of oneself, and thereby to find oneself.

He [the Christian] that is in all, and with all, can never be desolate. All the joys and all the treasures, and all the counsels and all the perfections, all the angels and all the saints of God are with him. All the kingdoms of the world and the glory of them are continually in his eye: the patriarchs, prophets and apostles are always before him. The councils and the fathers, the bishops and the doctors minister unto him. All temples are open before him, the melody of all choirs reviveth him, the learning of all universities doth employ him, the riches of all palaces delight him, the joys of Eden ravish him, the Revelations of St John transport him. The creation and the day of judgment please him, the hosannas of the Church militant, and the hallelujahs of the saints triumphant fill him, the splendour of all coronations entertain him, the joys of heaven surround him, and our saviour's cross like the centre of eternity is in him, it taketh up his thoughts, and exerciseth all the powers of his soul, with wonder, admiration, joy and thanksgiving. The omnipotence of God is his house, and eternity his habitation.[3]

Notes

1 Faith as a Question

1. Graham Greene, *Stamboul Train*, London 1932; collected edition, Heinemann/Octopus Books 1977, p. 288 (published in US by Viking Penguin Inc. under the title *Orient Express*).

2. Cf. J. Hick, *Faith and Knowledge*, London, Macmillan 1967; H. P. Owen, *The Christian Knowledge of God*, London, Athlone Press 1969; E. Maclaren, *The Nature of Belief*, London, Sheldon Press 1976; K. Ward, *The Concept of God*, London, Collins 1977.

3. Quoted by R. Gregor Smith in *J. G. Hamann*: *A Study in Christian Existence*, London, Collins 1960, p. 252.

4. Cf. J. Moltmann, *Theology of Hope*, London, SCM Press 1967; W. Pannenberg, *Basic Questions in Theology*, London, SCM Press, 1970 (vol. 1), 1971 (vol. 2), 1973 (vol. 3).

5. Karl Barth, *Church Dogmatics*, Vol. IV, part I, Edinburgh, T. & T. Clark 1956, p. 741.

6. Karl Barth, *Dogmatics in Outline*, London, SCM Press 1949, pp. 15f.

2 Faith as Human

1. John Macquarrie, *Christian Hope*, London, Mowbrays 1978, chapter 1.

2. Michael Polanyi, *Personal Knowledge*, London, Routledge and Kegan Paul 1958, pp. viif.

3. Ibid., p. 5.

4. H. H. Farmer, *Towards Belief in God*, Part I, London, SCM Press 1942, p. 25.

5. Ibid., p. 54.

6. W. Pannenberg, *The Apostles' Creed in the Light of Today's Questions*, London, SCM Press 1972, p. 3.

7. Ibid., p. 4.

8. Quoted by R. Gregor Smith in *J. G. Hamann*: *A Study in Christian Existence*, p. 57.

3 Faith as Trust

1. Dietrich Bonhoeffer, *Letters and Papers from Prison*, London, SCM Press, revised and enlarged edition 1971, pp. 347f.
2. Martin Luther, 'Preface to the Epistle to the Romans (1522)', *Works of Martin Luther*, Philadelphia, Mulkenberg Press 1932, p. 452.
3. Hans Küng, *On Being a Christian*, London, Collins 1977, p. 584.
4. Ibid., p. 589.

4 Faith as a Gift

1. David Hume, *Enquiry Concerning the Human Understanding*, ed., L. A. Selby-Biggs, Oxford, Oxford University Press 1902, p. 131.
2. John Oman, *Grace and Personality*, London, Cambridge University Press 1919, p. 129.
3. Rudolf Bultmann, *Faith*, London, A. & C. Black 1961, p. 69.
4. R. Gregor Smith, *Secular Christianity*, London, Collins 1966, p. 45.
5. Gerhard Ebeling, *The Nature of Faith*, London, Collins 1961 esp. chs 4 and 5.

5 Faith as Decision

1. 'The Disappearing God: A Discussion between J. P. Corbett, an agnostic and R. Gregor Smith, a Christian', *The Listener*, 21 January 1960, pp. 127–29.
2. Idem.
3. R. Gregor Smith, *The Free Man*, London, Collins 1960, p. 14.
4. John Macquarrie, *Christian Hope*, p. 25.
5. S. Kierkegaard, *Concluding Unscientific Postscript*, London, Oxford University Press 1941, p. 302.
6. Quoted by G. Ebeling in *The Nature of Faith*, p. 97.
7. C. S. Lewis, *Surprised by Joy*, London, Collins 1959, p. 189.

6 Faith as Confession

1. C. K. Barrett, *The Epistle to the Romans*, London, A. & C. Black 1962, p. 200.

7 Faith as Commitment

1. Bonhoeffer, *The Cost of Discipleship*, London, SCM Press 1959, p. 60.
2. Ibid., p. 72.
3. A. R. Johnson, *The Cultic Prophet in Israel's Psalmody*, Cardiff, University of Wales Press 1979.
4. See above p. 34.
5. Martin Luther, 'Preface to the Epistle to the Romans (1522)', pp. 451f.

6. John V. Taylor, *The Go-Between God,* London, SCM Press 1972, p. 98.

7. H. Butterfield, *Christianity and History*, London, Collins 1957, p. 189.

8   Faith as Freedom

1. Martin Heidegger, *Being and Time,* London, SCM Press 1962, p. 437.

2. Küng, *On Being a Christian*, p. 483.

3. One of the first to expound this view was the philosopher M. B. Foster in three essays in *Mind*, 1934–36.

9   Faith as Understanding

1. Martin Buber, *I and Thou*, Edinburgh, T. & T. Clark 1970, p. 85.

2. Peter Donovan, *Interpreting Religious Experience*, London, Sheldon Press 1979, p. 29.

3. St Augustine, *Commentary on the Gospel of John*, xxiv.6.

4. R. Gregor Smith, *Secular Christianity*, p. 46.

5. Gregor Smith, *The Doctrine of God,* London, Collins 1970, pp. 48f.

6. Polanyi, *Personal Knowledge*, pp. 198f.

10   Faith as Exploration

1. Bonhoeffer, *Letters and Papers from Prison*, revised and enlarged edition 1971, pp. 369f., letter to Eberhard Bethge 21 July 1944.

2. T. S. Eliot, 'Little Gidding', *The Complete Poems and Plays of T. S. Eliot*, London, Faber and Faber and New York, Harcourt Brace Jovanovich 1969, pp. 197f.

3. Thomas Traherne, *Centuries, Poems and Three Thanksgivings*.